A life less
ORDINARY

Allen Wood

UK Book Publishing.com

Editing, design, typesetting and publishing by UK Book Publishing

www.ukbookpublishing.com

ISBN: 978-1-918077-11-7

A life less
ORDINARY

CONTENTS

Introduction 1

Chapter 1 6

Chapter 2 9

Chapter 3 17

Chapter 4 29

Chapter 5 41

Chapter 6 53

Chapter 7 58

Chapter 8 77

Chapter 9 85

Chapter 10 115

Chapter 11 123

Chapter 12 134

Chapter 13 152

Chapter 14 180

Chapter 15 203

INTRODUCTION: WHO AM I?

⁓

I was born on 25th December 1959 in Galashiels, a town on the Scottish border's council area, south-eastern Scotland. It is on Gala Water near its junction with the river Tweed, 33 miles (53 km) south-southeast of Edinburgh. My mother *Cora Sheldrake,* a native of Galashiels, married my father *John Wood,* from Huddersfield, who at the time was working in the textile industry; however, in the early sixties the industry was in decline and many businesses were closing down. After I was born my parents, having been told they could not have any more children, adopted my brother Michael in 1963, and later that same year my father enlisted in the Army as prospects in Galashiels were not good. My father completed training in Catterick, Yorkshire in the Royal Signals and we moved to join him in 1964 when he was finally given married quarters. In 1965 we were posted to Herford, West Germany.

To my mother's surprise, having been told she could not have any more children, Angela, my sister, was born in 1966 and my brother Malcolm in 1970. In 1971 we were posted to Cyprus. Our posting to Cyprus was supposed to be for three years; however, with the turbulent political issues between the Turkish Cypriots and the Greek Cypriots, we often found ourselves stuck between fighting gangs with gunfire and bombs going off in our backyard, which as you can imagine for an 11 year old was quite frightening – although I do vividly recall one evening when a Greek restaurant directly opposite us was attacked and blown up. I recall my father running into my bedroom pulling me away from the window as I watched the attack unfold. Fortunately, in 1973 my father got an early promotion, and we were once again posted to Lippstadt, West Germany before the big battle for Cyprus erupted in 1974.

We remained in Germany until 1979 when my mother and father split up. I guess with four children and the constant unsettlement of moving home and schools it took its toll on the relationship and my mother moved to Spalding in Lincolnshire. In 1980 my father was promoted again to warrant officer and got another posting to the Dutch/German border area and finally left the army in 1981.

My childhood was that of a typical service lifestyle, often moving schools and having to make friends and start again every time we moved. I remember one time my father had been away a lot with the army, he had accumulated a number of weeks' leave, so much so that we decided to drive from Germany to Scotland. We were all packed into an estate car, my father, my mother, my two brothers and my sister, together with all the luggage to last the eight weeks or so we were away. On top of that 50% of the car was filled with 20ltr jerry cans full of petrol to last the journey. This was because as a service person in Germany you got very cheap fuel. So, you can imagine some 900 plus miles cramped into a car with the constant smell of petrol and horrible winding roads. That was just the start of my adventure and return to Bonny Scotland.

We arrived at my mother's sister's house early hours of the morning, and I recall my aunty Mona helping us in her nightgown. They lived in a small terrace council house in Whitecraig, Musselburgh.

My uncle Bill, aunty Mona, cousin Dave, Lynn and wee Billy plus the six of us. As you can imagine, a tight squeeze for 11 of us; the downside was myself and my cousin Dave were the eldest, so we naturally had to wait for the adults to go to bed before we got the use of the living room floor for our bed. I still have fond memories of the mischief we used to get up to during that visit. We would lie around with headphones on listening to music, The Rolling Stones, The Who, Nazareth to mention just a few, all vinyl of course; we would take it in turns to climb out of the blankets in the freezing cold to change the records. Dave was a bit of a practical joker, and my mother was not impressed one morning when she found the shampoo had been substituted with fairy liquid and the toothpaste with horseradish. Joy. Dave was quick to blame me, so I ended up having to wash all the dishes after tea that evening. No dishwashers in those days. Although it was fun spending time with my cousins, it was also very stressful. The length of the visit to my aunt's meant my parents had to put me into Musselburgh grammar school. This was, at the time, one of the roughest schools around. I'm not so sure this was a good thing. Firstly, Scottish education was far superior to what I had been used to, much more advanced, entering a classroom where everyone was doing algebra me not even knowing what it was made life very challenging to say the least. Secondly my English accent put me in a position I did not enjoy. I had a fight at school every day, so much so that one time I was given the cosh for fighting. This was a long leather belt which was forked at the end much like a lizard's tongue; you would hold your hands out, the belt was brought down with such force we were instructed to hold both hands out one to support the other from dropping during the punishment. I was petrified every day going to school. One time I overheard a group of boys saying they were going to get me after school the following day. That evening, I discussed with my cousin who had previously been to that school an escape route, so I didn't have to walk out the school gate. That day my cousin came to get me, and I climbed over a school wall, and we ran home over a wee burn (small river) only to end up getting my school uniform covered in mud which culminated with the belt from my mother at home. It was always a no-win situation for me during that period. Probably why the Johnny Cash song "A Boy Named Sue" resonates with me.

GROWING UP WITH A SERVICE BACKGROUND

Military children are often referred to as military BRATs. In the 1920s, families who accompanied service members on overseas assignments were known as British Regiment Attached Traveller or BRAT. What people do not tend to often know is that BRAT is not used in a derogatory manner. BRAT is an acronym that stands for bravery, resilience, adaptability, and toughness. Because of their rough lifestyle, military children live up to each of those four words.

There are many pros and cons about being a child growing up in a service family. The pros I guess are the fact that you are forced into having to make friends quickly, the fact that you're only ever in one place for a few years means you start again every move, learning how to communicate and make friends each time. You swap and change teachers at school, each having a different methodology of teaching, so you adapt to these changes and become better at understanding and adapting to others' ways and how they depict things. Some would look at this as a con due to the uncertainty and breaks in routine, which can cause family members to experience high anxiety, depression, PTSD and long-term mental health and wellness injuries. I feel this is not the case. The uncertainty and breaks push you to be resilient. You quickly adapt to meeting new people and quickly learn how to initiate conversation to make friendships. The diversity of other religions, nationalities and ways of life is brought to the forefront early in your life and you develop a skill of how to deal with them.

I recall one time whilst working with BP in Algeria some of the office staff said to me, Allen, we often see you outside talking to the gardener, you don't speak Arabic or French and he doesn't speak French or English, yet you always seem to understand his needs and always resolve his issues. I put this down to the communication skills learned by being a service child and forced into such diverse arenas. I believe this upbringing is the backbone of why and how I reacted and coped in my life's experiences.

* * *

CHAPTER 1

My final school days were completed from Kings School Gutersloh in Germany. After leaving school at 17 from the sixth form and still living in Lippstadt, Germany, I took a job as an apprentice vehicle mechanic. I got the job in a German garage because of my ability to speak German and the owner of the garage had several British customers, so I was useful for translating for them. I found it very difficult going to day release German school and trying to learn an apprenticeship totally in German. My friends who left school with me were earning three times what I was getting doing window cleaning, so as you can imagine it wasn't long before I opted out of my apprenticeship and onto window cleaning. It also meant I was now working with my friends, so this made life so much better. Especially in a foreign land.

During my school years I had learned how to play the guitar, and we formed a band called Atlas, named due to the mixture of the band members. One Scot, two English and one German / Dutch. We would play at the military sergeants' mess and officers' mess parties and youth club events etc. This was during the mid-seventies when you had long hair, shirt collars that would lift you off the ground on a windy day and three button high waisted flared trousers where you could take ten paces before your trousers moved. I had shoulder length hair in a feather cut with a beaded necklace. I would often see my father shake his head when I went out, wondering where he had gone wrong. I played football for the local town and was proud of being on TV during our games. I was always fit and enjoyed sports immensely. I held all the records at school for the 800 and 1500 metres and used to run for the school at cross country. I was enjoying life then. Money coming in and everything to play for.

My father was a keen caravanner. He loved driving, and living in Germany meant the world was so accessible by road. We would often travel to other countries, particularly Serbia and Montenegro or as it was known then Yugoslavia. I loved the water. In fact, during our time in Cyprus I joined the British Sub Aqua Club in RAF Akrotiri and became one of the youngest dive members. I used to train the squaddies in snorkel diving prior to them joining the club. To date this is my favourite hobby.

Anyway, the reason I mentioned that is because of my swimming abilities. I remember one time on holiday we went out to a remote island about 1.5 miles out to sea in our small dinghy which only had a 10hp engine attached to the rear, the intention being to spend the day and picnic on our own island. Unfortunately, whilst on the island the weather started to turn bad, so my father decided to ship us back, but as it had taken three trips to get us all out there, we were on a race against time to get back before the weather was too bad. After taking my mother and brother and lots of the equipment back to the mainland he came out again with me to pick up my sister, brother and the rest of the kit but unfortunately the weather turned so bad we were unable to get back to the mainland. As we approached the island, the waves being so rough ended up pushing our dinghy up against the rocks and we struggled to get ashore, so we opted to swim using fins, mask and snorkel and pull the boat behind us. At least that way we could get on firm ground then pull the boat in with the ropes. During the struggle to get onto the island, dragging the boat behind us, the waves pushed the boat which was now full of water and trapped my father's leg against the sharp rocks lacerating his leg and causing it to bleed quite badly. We finally got to shore and dragged what was left of the inflatable boat onto the island. We overnighted on the island using the boat as shelter. My mother was obviously distraught on the mainland wondering what had happened to us. She managed to get all the campers on the mainland to drive their cars to the beach and switch the lights on to see if they could see us. No one knew if we were still on the island or not, but there was nothing anyone could do. The weather was so bad the waves were so big that other boats were unable to come and help. We spent that night huddled together trying to keep warm. The following morning after a horrendous night the weather was good and the water was calm so as dawn came, I put on my mask and snorkel and I swam back the one and half miles to the mainland, and got help to bring back my father, sister and the remains of the boat. I recall my mother's face when I appeared – she had not slept a wink and was distraught, having thought we had perished in the storm. My experience of being one of the youngest divers when we were in Cyprus certainly helped give me the confidence for the one-and-a-half-mile swim in open water that day.

* * *

CHAPTER 2

During our time in Cyprus, we had made lots of friends, both Greek Cypriot and Turkish Cypriot. Our Turkish Cypriot friends called Dr Teken and Mary who was an Irish girl were close neighbours of ours and when the troubles started Dr Teken moved his wife Mary and children back to the UK for safety. It was not so easy for him as he didn't have a British passport, so found himself unable to remain in the UK. I later moved to Dagenham and stayed with them for some time whilst starting an apprenticeship as an electrician. I completed my course and exams from Peterborough skill centre before moving to Spalding to stay with my mother. It was during this time that I became interested in joining the Royal Marines.

I had completed my apprenticeship and finished my electrical qualifications but couldn't find work as an electrician in Spalding. Spalding is in Lincolnshire and is predominantly farming land. It's as flat as a pancake for as far as the eye can see. I ended up working in a sugar beet factory just labouring solely to give me an income. I used to keep fit and go out running most days. I often used to pass a guy who lived not so far away. He always wore a shirt with Royal Marines Commando written on the back. One day on my run he caught up with me and asked me if I'd ever considered joining the Marines. I hadn't even heard of them. Having talked with him in depth I decided to look at it in a bit more detail. What grabbed my attention was the fact that they were known to have some of the hardest training in the military: 36 weeks of basic training before even getting into the Marines and only when you pass and you're in does the real training start. This sounded like the challenge I was up for. I recall walking into the Royal Navy and Royal Marines careers office in Peterborough and one of the staff jumped up and said would you like to join the Navy, lad. No, I replied, I'd like to join the Marines. Christ, he said, not that lot you must be crazy, are you sure? And he tried to persuade me the Navy would be better. But this only encouraged me even more to join the Marines. After my interview I was told there would be a fitness test at one of their centres and provided I passed that I would be invited for a selection course at Lympstone Commando Training Centre; if I passed that I would then be able to join and start training.

A week later I successfully completed my first fitness test at the centre and was given a card with exercises to do to get myself ready for the selection test at Lympstone Commando Training Centre. I was told it would be about six weeks before the next space was available. Two weeks later I received a phone call asking if I would attend a three-day selection course at Lympstone. I think because I got top marks in fitness, I was moved up the queue.

I remember receiving my travel tickets and getting on the train to the commando centre. The train leaves from Exeter St David's to Lympstone Commando Training Centre, known as CTCRM (Commando Training Centre Royal Marines). It was a very small three carriage train and when it pulled into CTCRM it was a tiny platform which resembled a bus stop at the bottom of a field with a guarded fence and an obstacle course of walls and high ropes etc. It looked so intimidating. I was met by a Royal Marine who called out my name and marched me up to my accommodation. I was given a brief on timings, shown where the galley was for meals and told to await the arrival of others before a start would be made on our assessments.

I spent three days being run off my feet. Our very first test we had to run 1.5 miles in sub nine minutes 30 seconds before we moved on. The guys who failed this were sent back home immediately. Physical tests every day with some breaks where we would be introduced to life as a Royal Marine and some history of the corps. On my journey back home, I remember being in total bewilderment at what I'd just experienced. I was given my results before leaving CTCRM and told I had come joint first in my assessment and that I should keep training and await my joining instructions.

All potential recruits take a Defence Aptitude Assessment and are interviewed at the Armed Forces Careers Office to assess their suitability. A series of physical assessments are conducted including a sight test and medical examination. Then the Pre-Joining Fitness Test Plus (PJFT+). The PJFT+ is a circuit assessment. You then have to complete the circuit three times, with each requiring the completion of 20 burpees, 30 sit ups, 20 press ups and a one-minute plank. On completion of the three circuits, you are required to perform a set of five pull ups.

The final selection assessment for potential recruits is the Candidate Preparation Course; this lasts three days and assesses physical ability and intellectual capacity to undertake the training. That's the time when you first see CTCRM, and you step off the train into a world of pain. That's exactly what it was when I first set eyes on the bottom field.

Royal Marines Commando Training is one of the world's longest and most arduous training programmes. The programme is intended to train you in all skills required to become an amphibious soldier with the Marines.

Once through the recruiting process, you are given a date to start Initial Training at Commando Training Centre Royal Marines (CTCRM), Lympstone. Initial training is a five-stage process, with only successful candidates progressing to the next stage.

The first of these stages is a four-week Recruit Orientation Phase (ROP). I remember this stage very well. Straight from civilian life the first stop was the barber. You're called in and you sit on the chair and the nice man makes small talk with you. Then he asks you what you would like. He takes his time discussing which bits you'd like left long and the exact style you'd like. Then after all that detail he just shaves your head. You just sit there and think what am I doing? This stage provides an introduction to life as a marine and includes Physical Training (PT) and swimming sessions and testing, drill and personal administration, weapon handling, close combat training and basic fieldcraft. ROP culminates in a three-day field exercise and fitness assessment.

The sense of pride and accomplishment after completing the ROP was overwhelming. Yet, I knew this was just the beginning of what would be an arduous and transformative journey. The physical and mental challenges faced were numerous, but they only strengthened my resolve to become part of the Royal Marines Commando.

Initial training began with a four-week orientation phase, which was designed to acclimate recruits to military life. The physical training was intense and exhausting, but it was just a taste of what was to come. We were introduced to basic fieldcraft, weapon handling, close combat training, and swimming sessions. The culmination of this phase was a three-day field exercise and a fitness assessment, which we had to pass to progress further.

You have two attempts to pass this assessment. If successful, you move on to spend a further 32 weeks in training. This first part clears out a high percentage of those who just can't handle it. It's especially daunting because this part is just the selection before kick-off.

PHASE 1 – 10 WEEKS

Individual skills

Having completed the ROP, you continue training by learning and developing more individual skills. You continue with: PT gym sessions, swimming sessions, drill, weapon handling and fieldcraft, but also develop map reading and navigation skills, live firing experience and marksmanship training.

This culminates in a fitness assessment and the field exercise known as the 'Baptist Run' for obvious reasons. We are, after all, new babies.

PHASE 2 – 13 WEEKS

Team and Section Skills (weeks 11 to 15)

At this stage training progresses to learning skills that include Reconnaissance and Surveillance (RS), small team tactics, tactical navigation and signalling, medic training and section tactics. PT and swimming sessions continue. You are constantly running around, keeping up your fitness levels.

Troop and Urban Skills (weeks 16 to 23)

In this final stage of the initial training you progress to more targeted combat training, comprising: General Purpose Machine Gun (GPMG), pistol handling and live firing, troop tactics, tactical night navigation, Royal Marines close combat training, close quarter battle training and Strike Operations (Strike Ops) training. This was a very scary but exciting part of my training. Well, they say training – there is no holding back here when fighting, many come away with black eyes and cuts and breaks.

PHASE 3 – 8 WEEKS

Commando Phase (weeks 24 to 31)

In your Commando phase, you are not allowed to walk anywhere during the whole eight weeks. If you are seen walking at any time by any staff in CTCRM, you will end up with extra physical punishment. In this stage, you lose the black beret and wear a commando hat which is not too dissimilar to a beany – that distinguishes you to everyone in Lympstone so you can be easily identified if walking.

If successful in the first stages of training, you will progress to introductory Commando training. This is when you undertake: Live firing tactical training - at section and troop level, day and night manoeuvre training and amphibious foundation training. A final exercise and four Commando tests will follow:

The endurance course: Two miles of tunnels, pools, streams, bogs and woods, followed by a four-mile run back to camp where you will need to achieve six out of ten in a shooting test. This is conducted under pressure and before you have time to slow your heart rate down from the endurance course you've just endured.

The nine-mile speed march: This needs to be completed in 90 minutes, as a unified squad, while carrying 30lbs of equipment and rifle.

The problem is if you sustain an injury that needs time to heal you end up getting back trooped whilst you wait to heal. Nobody wants this because it just prolongs your time in training. You lose the friends you joined with and end up joining the next troop that is coming through behind you. Most people try to hide any injuries to avoid this. At the end of this phase, you have your bottom Field pass out and test exercise. This is a big test which a lot of people fail. Only 20% of the guys I joined with got through this part the first time.

The Tarzan assault course: This is an aerial assault course which needs to be completed in 13 minutes, while carrying 30lbs of equipment and rifle and ends with a 30ft rope climb. You must touch the top eye of the rope and call out your personal number before the clock stops.

The 30-mile march: This is a march across Dartmoor, which needs to be completed in less than eight hours, carrying 40lbs of equipment and a rifle. They always find you the boggiest part of Dartmoor to do this just to make sure you're wet through and tired – no point making it easy for you.

KING'S SQUAD – 1 WEEK

The 'King's Squad' is the culmination of 32 weeks' Royal Marines Commando Training and a tradition that has been in place since

His Majesty King George V granted the honour in 1918. At pass out this is when you become a Royal Marine Commando and are awarded the coveted Green Beret. You then move into the real training when you join a commando unit and start again from the bottom of the ladder.

* * *

CHAPTER 3

It was three weeks after passing my selection when I received my joining instructions. I was given a limited list of clothing and items I could bring. It was evident from the list that I would not be needing any glad rags as they say because for the next 36 weeks, I would be either too busy or too exhausted to worry about socialising. The average Royal Marine recruit can expect to receive around four to six hours of sleep per night; there's a reason that they're known as 'nods' – due to a combination of huge physical exertion and sleep deprivation, recruits will frequently 'nod off'.

The eerie feeling of arriving at CTCRM will never leave me. All your training has been towards earning the green beret and when you march up and collect it, from that moment on you become taller and much more confident; it's a memory that will always be with you. The pain and resilience just to get there. I could write a separate book on the experience of Royal Marine Training; it's known as one of the toughest military training regimes for a reason.

But all that said and done, once you complete your basic training you get shipped out to join a commando unit and this is when the real training starts. Basic training is just preparation for this stage. It means you're now fit enough and competent enough to start becoming a commando.

Figure 1 CTCRM Bottom Field

Figure 2 Regain Training

Figure 3 Fireman's carry

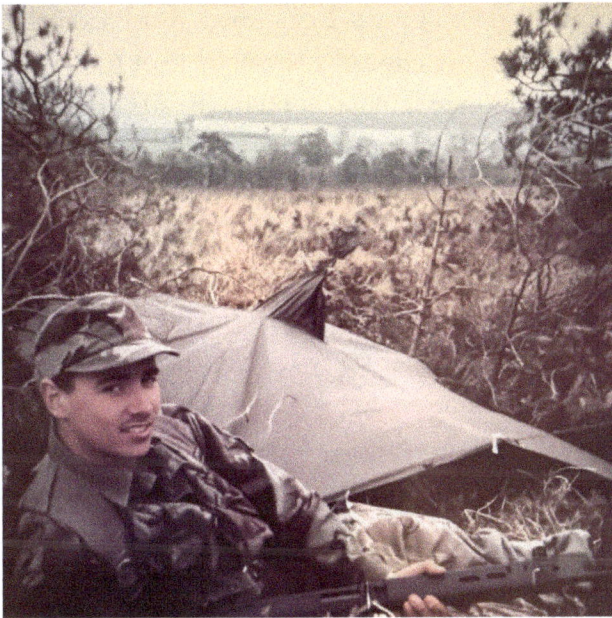

Figure 4 How to make a shelter with poncho

Figure 5 Passing out of CTCRM

My first commando unit was 42 Commando at Bickleigh Barracks, Plymouth, sited on the edge of Dartmoor. Not too far away from Dartmoor prison, quite famous in many movies. The idea was that to escape from Dartmoor prison was the easy part, getting across the bleak Dartmoor swamps was the challenge. The weather on Dartmoor can turn very quickly and you can easily get lost in the Dartmoor mist and end up chest deep in marsh. But this was now my new home. Armed with my kit bag full of what little belongings I had I entered yet another scary first. Although I was officially a Royal Marine commando, for the old sweats here, I was still very much a recruit. I was assigned to 6 troop L company and given my bed space and locker. There were four to a room and I unpacked and waited for my fate.

I joined 42 Commando after a short break from CTCRM. I reported in on the Sunday and the other Marines in my room had obviously been away for the weekend. I had got there Sunday morning early so as not to start on the wrong foot. I had unpacked my kit and had everything in my locker folded to globe and laurel size all Percy perfect. In training your locker had to always be immaculate and was frequently checked for anything not perfect and the whole locker was tipped out and you had to start again if the slightest thing was out of place. The Royal Marines have a magazine called Globe and Laurel which symbolizes our cap badge. All our clothes in training had to be folded to the same size as the Globe and Laurel and the magazine was used as a measure.

Our cap badge has a meaning. The Lion and Crown denotes a 'Royal' regiment. Admiral Lord St Vincent, recognising the great service which the Corps had given to that point, recommended to King George III that they should be given this title. It was granted to the Corps by Royal Command on 29th April 1802.

Laurel Wreath: It is generally accepted, but not certain, that the Laurel Wreath was awarded to the Corps by the French in recognition of the gallantry of the Marines at the battle and capture of Belle Isle in 1761.

The Globe: in 1827 HRH The Duke of Clarence presented new Colours to all the Grand Divisions. In doing so he announced that HM King George IV had directed that the difficulty of selecting Battle Honours amidst so many glorious deeds was too great, so the Corps should have the 'Great Globe itself' as its emblem on the crest, to be surrounded by the Laurel Wreath. The Globe also represents the fact that Royal Marines were, and still are, involved in conflicts all around the world.

The Foul Anchor incorporated into the emblem in 1747, the Foul Anchor (an anchor entangled in a rope) is the badge of the

Lord High Admiral and indicates that the Corps is part of the Royal Navy.

It was later that afternoon that the "old sweats", a term used for long serving Marines, started to return to barracks. I remember being very nervous and sceptical of what I might be faced with, but to my surprise I was welcomed warmly by them. There is something about earning the green beret that commands a certain amount of respect, and this was clear from the open welcome I received from other members of 6 Troop L Company. That said, it wasn't too long before someone said: you don't have to have your locker like you're still in training. Your locker now belongs to you, no one goes near it. That became obvious as I could see the pictures of Page 3 girls pinned to the inside doors of their lockers. It felt good and I felt part of the family.

I soon got into the routine. Every morning there would be a stand to. The troop would parade outside at 08:00 in PT kit and we would always do physical fitness first. It varied between long runs and circuit training, but everything had a competitive edge.

The unit was preparing for mountain training as this is part of the build-up before going to Norway on Arctic training, so after sport we would get into uniform and start the build-up. Usually followed by lectures on survival in the mountains. Putting up cover and tying knots. These lectures were run by the mountain and Arctic warfare group called the cadre. Mountain Leaders are an elite cadre of Royal Marines who are experts in long range reconnaissance, Arctic warfare and mountain climbing. Cold weather survival and operations and cliff assaults. As their primary peacetime role is to teach their techniques to other Royal Marines and share their expertise with other military units such as the SAS etc.

Like I said earlier, the real training starts at a commando unit. I was now being trained how to survive in the Arctic. This training was to last several months and over several arduous exercises and various arenas from the wet Pen y Fan in Wales in winter, to the high mountains in Kinlochleven, Scotland – or kill lochleven as we called it. I'll always remember my first night exercise in the freezing winter, my legs feeling like lead from carrying a heavy pack up such a vertical climb then the tactical night descent. We had to abseil off the side of the mountain using the free roping style. This is where there are no carabiners: the rope simply wraps around your body, and you pull it forward to slow your descent. It was raining and slippery. I took my rope from the mountain leader and started my backward abseil. Suddenly I started to fall fast. The rope was not in my hand, and I was unable to slow my fall. Fortunately, I still had hold of the rope with my left hand, and I was frantically swinging my right arm as shown in training to find the rope. Eventually I got it and pulled it forward. It felt like I was cut in half as it stopped me about five feet from the deck. I was still new, and all this was tactical which meant done in silence, I thought I was a dead man for a minute. This was another type of training altogether.

The first week, which forms the basic mountain training, started with a chance to refresh navigation skills whilst increasing duration and elevation of routes, with increasing weight to bear. Interspersed with the daily marches, briefs were delivered on topics such as long-range communications equipment, kit preparation and mountain tactics. Then weapons and ammunition scales get added to the already-heavy loads, building an appreciation for what it means to act as small teams in the challenging mountainous environment. The skills and tactics in mountain warfare differ from those in other environments and need to be practised to achieve success in mountain operations.

The nature of the ground sometimes presents obstacles, such as river crossings and cliff faces, and we were shown how to tackle these. Surveillance and reconnaissance training also forms an integral part of mountain training. To be able to survive in and fight in some of the most inhospitable conditions, commandos fundamentally have to sustain a higher level of resilience. It's an inescapable fact that this means hardening yourself through arduous training; this is exactly what mountain training offers. The progression from my basic training through to the preparation for my introduction to Arctic training was immense.

The Arctic: First, those who are new to the Arctic must undergo a series of intensive trials to ensure they are able to survive – building shelters, living off the land and dealing with cold shock during the infamous ice breaking drills, which involves being plunged into a hole in the ice and climbing out of the water unassisted using ski poles. I recall this first part of my Arctic training with vivid detail. The training staff keeping you in the water asking you to recite your name and number and other more thought-provoking questions. All this is designed to keep you focused. Getting yourself out was not so easy either. The shock of the freezing water hitting you then the process of getting your pack off, then the skis out and finally using the ski poles to drag yourself out. The reason for using the poles is because sometimes the gap between the water and ice can be quite high and trying to climb out onto ice can be very difficult and with the effect of the cold you very quickly become overwhelmed, exhausted and hypothermia starts to set in, so getting it right is critical. Of course, once you're out you then have the task of getting out of wet clothes and into dry ones. This has to be done fast as the cold and windchill factor can quickly send you into a downward spiral. As the wind increases, it draws heat from the body, driving down skin temperature and eventually the internal body temperature. Therefore, the wind makes it FEEL much colder.

If the temperature is -18°C and the wind is blowing at 15 mph, the wind chill is -28°C. So, speed is of the essence. This brutal part of the training is designed to help you recognise and reduce the risks of cold shock: a physical response to being immersed in cold water that can rapidly incapacitate and even kill.

Crossing a frozen lake or river can bring a tactical advantage but comes at significant risk, so ice breaking is about preparing for being suddenly dropped into bracing water. After rewarming from the dip through the ice, we go on the survival course and head into the wilderness to construct and inhabit survival shelters. Half the battle is managing the climate and the terrain. Snowstorms can occur suddenly, so learning the basics of survival is key to operating in the Arctic conditions. The Cold Weather Warfare Course has three phases – survival, mobility and warfare. This creates a well-rounded winter warrior, enabling you to operate effectively in this unforgiving environment. Of course, all this sounds exciting but when you can't even ski to start with you can imagine the challenges.

The learning to ski side I remember as fun. We were given three weeks to master the art of skiing. How to herringbone on the way up and snow plough on the way down. You would learn about balance and how leaning your shoulder forward would change your direction depending on which shoulder you used, left or right. After about a week you were feeling very confident skiing and started progressing with speed, even showing off a little. Just when you thought you had mastered it, they give you a nice heavy pack to carry. Everything to do with balance you thought you had mastered goes out the window and once again you find yourself face down in the snow. The fun side was looking at it from the outside – it was like a comedy sketch with bodies in various positions falling all over the slopes. Frustratingly dusting themselves down and starting again, over and over again. But eventually you do get it, and it falls into place.

The military ski is specially designed between a downhill ski and a cross-country ski. Downhill skiing happens on a slant, and the ski is wider, your feet are locked in place forcing you into a position, while cross-country skiing Nordic style is done on flatter ground, the ski is a lot thinner and your feet are only fixed to the ski from the toe – the heel is free to lift off the ski. While Nordic style takes place on relatively flat terrain, with only gradual inclines and declines or undulating hills, alpine style takes place on downhill slopes. These slopes can often at times be very steep and contain challenging elements like jumps or moguls. Military skiing needs to provide both flat terrain and slopes, so the ski is slightly wider than a cross-country ski but still allows the heel to be lifted off the ski. The ability to lift your heel is crucial when carrying a lot of weight and a weapon. You can imagine if your feet were locked in position and both skis together like you travel on a hard compact slope, then suddenly you hit soft undulating snow, you would very quickly end up face down in the snow having been catapulted forward with the sudden slowing down as you hit the soft snow and the weight of your pack propelling you forward. You would most certainly cause yourself an injury. During this phase of Arctic training, you will see many a commando sporting a black eye, broken nose or chipped tooth where he has not yet mastered the telemark element of this type of skiing, and as your weapon is being carried across your chest it simply bounces up and alters your rugged good looks. To avoid this, you must push one ski forward from the other, almost making it one long ski and you must bend and relax your knees. This is called telemark style. To do this you must be able to lift your heel off the ski. Hence why military skiing is so specialised.

A Royal Marine is not classed as Arctic trained until he has completed three winters in the Arctic, mastered the art of living above the treeline in snow holes, and is competent enough to be able to navigate the land. Navigation in the snow is a whole different ball game. Out on the moors or on the mountains when you look at a map you can very quickly see exactly where you are by the contour lines on the map, which very clearly shows you the undulating peaks and troughs. Or streams and lakes can be easily identified. Now picture this on a land full of snow, all the peaks and troughs have gone, flattened and smoothed over with a bed of snow. It is impossible to see where the hill starts or even how steep it is. More so if it's snowing – when the snow meets the land it causes a white out, so you find it extremely difficult to navigate. You don't know if you're crossing a field or a lake. No more contours, streams or hill to identify, nothing but a white canvas. A whiteout is when, in poor weather, the sky and ground become one so there is no horizon line, and it is impossible to make out the lay of the land just in front of you. It can be very intimidating, especially around ridges, steep avalanche prone slopes and cornices (lips of compacted snow that overhang cliffs and outcrops). Without anything to aim a compass bearing at, you can drift significantly off course and the eyes and mind play tricks, especially if a strong wind is blowing snow diagonally across your route or into your face. Forget the old idea of throwing snowballs in front of you to aim on - it doesn't work.

Careful route planning is essential. Design a route using objectives that are changes in contour information which can provide physical feedback. For example, a straight-line bearing takes us diagonally downwards across a slope for 600m to reach flat ground. Using pacing and feeling the change in the contour spacing enables us to be reasonably accurate about our position. Further confirmation can be obtained by asking others to walk away in different directions to the limit of visibility and observe if they appear to be level, above or below. This idea can also help gauge the slope aspect (direction the slope is facing). Another way is by sending an individual to the limit of visibility then directing them left or right onto the bearing, then the group walks to them and the process is repeated.

This is a depressingly slow and cold process. Working as a team it is imperative you stay together and not lose sight of each other. Once you become isolated it is very easy to become lost and disoriented.

My first winter and Arctic introduction was successful, and I went on to complete three winters and I became a military ski instructor and enjoyed teaching new marines how to survive the Arctic challenges. It was my turn now to select the challenging routes the newbies would take when doing their tactical night ski introduction. We would make sure the route had hills and new snow to stumble upon. We would navigate the guys to the peak of the hill and in the black of night send them on their way to meet at a chosen rendezvous, but because it was tactical there was no noise to be made. It was extremely entertaining in the silence of the night – all you could hear is the swish of skis then a sudden muffled sound as they meet deep soft snow, and they haven't quite got the hang of telemark skiing. Black eyes, broken noses and fat lips were always on show at dawn turn out. Such fun.

* * *

CHAPTER 4

◁∽◁∽◁▷

We had just finished 15 days living above the treeline in snow holes on one of the biggest military exercises for decades on the northern flank of Norway. It was our time to come in and restock our resources. We were helicoptered by Sea King helicopter onto an American navy ship in the fjords. We were shown to some lower deck bunk beds where we could rest and get cleaned up and start our preparation for our next mission. Coming out of the cold from living in snow holes where the outside temperature can reach minus 30 degrees Celsius, the place felt roasting. Your face felt on fire despite other guys on the ship feeling the cold. We were walking around in tee shirts whilst most were layered up. If you pressed your thumb and forefinger together you could feel a slight pain behind the nails as your hands started to adapt to the warmth.

It wasn't long before an American naval officer caught up with us and ordered a couple of us to help out in the ship's galley. I couldn't believe, having been out in the thick of it for 15 days solid, to come in and find ourselves being assigned to pot wash duties on board a ship to help out. We had been in the galley just over an hour when our Colour Sergeant walked into the galley, he looked at us two in the pot wash area then looked over at the far side of the galley where there was an American sailor sat on a seat with his feet up on a table reading a paper. I could see it immediately on his face. He was livid. You two, he shouted, back to your bunks and rest up. The day my Marines come off a task and start cleaning up when some American sailor has his feet up doing fuck all, who hasn't even been out of his cosy warm shit hole, will be a dark day.

If you were to sketch a figure of what you imagine a big ugly Scottish marine was to look like you would come up with Mac, our Colour Sergeant, he was around 6'4" with hands like shovels, a pitted face and the spitting image of Desperate Dan out of The Beano. You do not want to be on the wrong side of that man mountain. Needless to say, we were grateful he was one of ours. We could hear his raised voice as he dressed down the ship's officer who sent us to do the extra works.

I will never forget my first time being on the wrong side of our Colour Sergeant. I was still a newbie in 42 Commando and was a little short of cash. As a marine you get four travel warrants a year to allow you to travel to see your family. My mother at the time lived in Stornoway on the Isle of Lewis. On my first trip home I received £400 from my travel warrant. This was due to the travel distance between Plymouth and Stornoway. Being naive and short of cash I suggested to Taff my mate that we should each put in a travel warrant for Stornoway. When we handed it in to get approval we were called into the office and handed them back with the comment: Take these away and rethink them, lads. With a convincing look we said, "Why, sir, what's the problem?" Are you saying you both went to Stornoway on the same weekend in two separate cars? Obviously as we were already committed, we replied yes, sir, we each had a car full and travelled up together for an engagement party. Are you sure because to me it stinks? No, sir, it's true. Okay came the reply, be it on your heads.

That was mistake number one. Not having expected our submission to be challenged we quickly got together to go through the whole trip. Who sat where in each car, where we stopped for fuel, where we got the ferry from and to, what time the ferry set sail and everything we could think of if challenged. Later that day we were summoned into the commanding officer's office. Taff first, he was in the office for around 15 minutes whilst I stood outside going through every inch of the trip in my head. Taff came out and I was sent in. Right, said our CO, are you sticking to your travel warrant claim or would you like me to return it to you? No sir, it's correct. I would like to stick with it. Feeling very confident we had covered everything. Okay, he said, picking up the phone to talk to the SIB (Special investigation Branch). Putting his hand over the telephone mic he once again said, I'll give you one more chance to give in and take back your claim, but before you answer know this: Taff docked off the ferry three hours after you. My whole world just fell out of the sky, of all the silly mistakes we forgot to discuss the docking times. Bugger. Ahh I see, sir, well in that case please may I have my travel warrant returned so I may reconsider it. With that I was dismissed. On my way out the CO said, send in your Colour Sergeant. Oh shit.

We were sat upstairs in our room when we heard the holler of Mac's voice, Wood, Barrett out here now.

Our Colour Sergeant had been given instructions to take us on a refresher of unarmed combat training. Needless to say, Taff and I received a proper painful reminder of unarmed combat training with no holds barred, by one of the toughest marines we ever had the pleasure of meeting, followed by several guard duties on the wet horrible exercises to follow. After which Mac said, next time you want to rob the corps you come see me first, I know how it works. I did not envy the American officer now on the receiving end of that man. We remained on board for two days and were assigned to the ship's Seal team to help pave the way for a night grounding. The American Seals were a good bunch; it was interesting working with them. They certainly had all the best kit, but boy did they have a lot to learn about Arctic warfare.

I recall setting off as an eight-man team getting into the small rigid raiders and beaching in the dark. Our job was to lay a route for the rest of the assigned deployment to follow; we marked out the route with Cyalume sticks for the other troops to follow. Unfortunately, the area we were assigned was not the best. It was a steep climb up the side of a mountain. Our route selection had to take into consideration it was for a good 100+ soldiers to follow on skis – this required a tight line of traversing the mountain, making it a long tiresome start for the boys. Once the path was marked, we moved up above the treeline again and awaited the deployment of the troops covering their advance from above. Because of the time this would take, we dug in snow holes so we could get a warm drink and some food. Snow holes are a great shelter provided you dig them correctly. They are usually dug into the side of the mountain. First you must dig down before digging up, in order to construct a cold air trench – as you know, hot air rises, cold air falls, so you dig your sleeping platform above the cold air trench. Another important factor is oxygen – you can imagine a snow hole with three or four men in could quickly deplete the oxygen. You would make the roof of your snow hole as smooth as possible to prevent drips forming and making you wet inside whilst cooking. You would have a ski pole poked through the roof to allow oxygen in. This would require intermittent moving to keep the hole from clogging up if snowing outside. If it was 30 degrees below outside, lighting a candle in the snow hole can bring the temperature up to zero degrees which will feel quite warm. It was interesting chatting to the Seals on various war stories while we waited. It was amusing as we helped them understand the importance of dehydrating their food in the Arctic as they crunched away at partially dehydrated food. This was clearly an environment they were unfamiliar with.

After a couple of hours, we were told that we would be collected by a Sea King helicopter to be dropped off at our next objective in the exercise. When the chopper arrived, I was given the headset to talk to the pilots as we discussed our new grid reference. The headsets are great as no one but the pilots and you can hear what's being said. Being British and a British naval helicopter pilot we were both on the same wavelength of humour. I see you have the privilege of working with the American elite, said the pilot in a sarcastic manner. Shall we have a little fun with them? I laughed knowing exactly what he was talking about. During our various training scenarios, we have to be aware of helicopter ditching. This is usually done in an adapted environment where the helicopter is ditched into a deep pool, and you practise the technique of getting out of a ditched chopper. Although you are prepared for it and there are divers in the water for emergencies, it's still quite frightening and some people do not react well at all. So, the pilot suggested an imitation fall from the sky manoeuvre. I signalled over to the other marine with us, and he gripped the sides, knowing what was to come. The Seals were all chatting amongst themselves totally oblivious to what was about to happen. The pilot dropped the Sea King so fast it literally gave you butterflies as you were lifted off your feet. The squeals coming from the Seals was the centre of many a ribbing for the rest of our time together. But all said and done, they were a good bunch to work with despite their lack of Arctic experience.

Figure 6 Learning to ski in Norway

Figure 7 Building up confidence skiing before heavy packs are introduced

Figure 8 Norway wilderness

Figure 9 Brushwood shelter

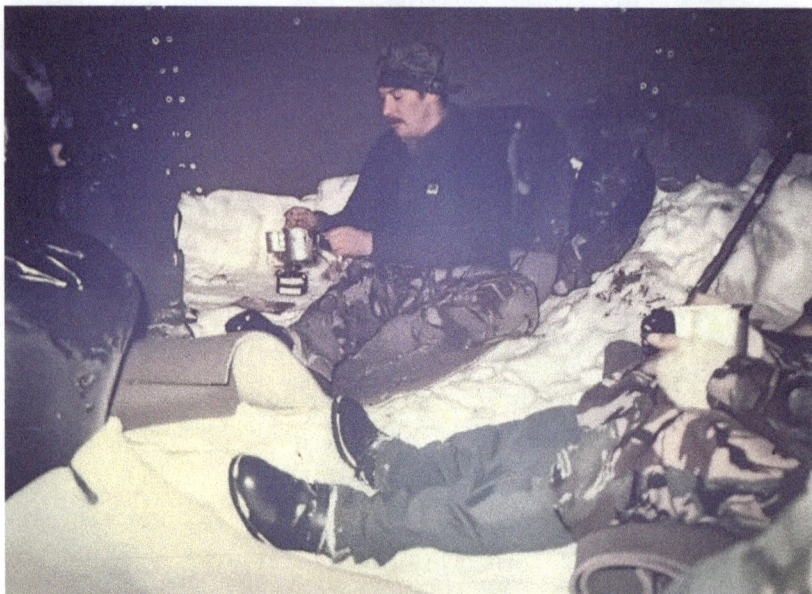

Figure 10 Inside Brushwood / Tent sheet shelter

Figure 11 Snow holes

Figure 12 Snow shelters

Figure 13 Breaking Ice drills

Figure 14 Preparing Snow Holes

Figure 15 Norway Nights outside snow holes

Figure 16 Inside Snow Hole

Figure 17 Bed area in snow hole

Figure 18 Time to rest in snow hole

* * *

CHAPTER 5

After 15 weeks in the Arctic it was time to get back home to Bickleigh Barracks and prepare for our tour in Northern Ireland. Urban warfare is another challenge to overcome in the never-ending training demands of being one of Britain's elite soldiers.

The nice thing about coming back to the UK is the greenery when you fly in and see all the green fields and trees. It's such a sight. Particularly when all you've seen for the past four months is white cold snow. However, no time to rest on our laurels as they say, nothing short of a long weekend leave then back to the grindstone. For me it was another first as we started our beat up for our next deployment. Urban warfare and tactics. In training we brush over it with some close quarter battle training in Tregantle Fort Cornwall. Tregantle Fort in southeast Cornwall is one of several forts surrounding Plymouth that were built to deter the French from attacking naval bases on the Channel coast. Close quarter battle (CQB) in training was great fun but nothing like I was about to experience in a commando unit.

Urban warfare is warfare in urban areas such as towns and cities. Urban combat differs from combat in the open at both operational and the tactical levels. Complicating factors in urban warfare include the presence of civilians and the complexity of the urban terrain. Fighting in urban areas negates the advantages that one side may have over the other in armour, heavy artillery, or air support. Ambushes laid down by small groups of enemy with handheld anti-tank weapons can destroy entire columns of modern armour, while artillery and air support can be severely reduced to limit civilian casualties as much as possible; in fact, civilians are often used as shields. Some civilians may be difficult to distinguish from such combatants as armed militias and gangs, and particularly individuals who are simply trying to protect their homes from attackers. Tactics are complicated by a three-dimensional environment, limited fields of view and fire because of buildings, enhanced concealment and cover for defenders, below-ground infrastructure, and the ease of placement of booby traps and snipers. The PIRA (The Provisional Irish Republican Army – the result of a split in the Irish Republican Army (IRA) which occurred in 1969) used this type of tactic against the British army in Northern Ireland. An improvised explosive device (IED) attack is the use of a "homemade" bomb and/or destructive device to destroy, incapacitate, harass, or distract. IEDs are used by criminals, vandals, terrorists, suicide bombers, and insurgents. They also used hit and run tactics using snipers. Ambushes, vehicle check points, raids and sabotage. They reigned with terror to intimidate local civilians using tar and feathering to anyone suspected of aiding British forces personnel. Guerrilla warfare at its worst. The first thing on my mind is: how on earth do you combat this sort of enemy?

We have a saying in the Marines called the seven Ps. Prior Planning and Preparation Prevents Piss Poor Performance. So, preparation it is. We have six months before our deployment and our expected deployment will be six months on the ground. Our beat up was both physical and mentally challenging, a mixture of lectures in understanding our enemy, the environment we would be operating in and the dos and don'ts of urban challenges. This is another section of my life I could probably write a dedicated book on – so much to take in, understanding this type of battlefield.

The issue for training is how do you simulate urban street battles. A week in Whinney Hill gets you a tower-block. Copehill Down gets you rubbled streets and clutter. Corsham gets you underground and Longmoor has tightly packed terrace houses. No British training estate is large enough to look like a town. I will always remember after all the training and lessons we were tasked with a final exercise in The Sennybridge Training Area; this is a UK Ministry of Defence military training area near the village of Sennybridge in Powys, Wales. Our enemy was from 45 Commando who had come all the way from Scotland just to terrorise us. Nothing like getting your own to play the baddies. Why not? After all, they know all your tactics, your responses but most of all how to piss you off the best. Our training here lasted a week. This was nothing more than fun for the boys from 45 Commando because they were allowed to be dressed in plain clothes, party the night away and get amongst us causing a riot. What a great job. They would be given tasks to disrupt us. I recall doing a night patrol and listening to the party at full blast. The boys had a detachment of Wrens with them as the females in the make-believe town. WRNS (wrens) stands for Women's Royal Naval Service. Being as Royal Marines come under the Navy command, Wrens are often used to help out. This was all well and good, but it did encourage the lads to show off a bit and really make our lives grim. One of the lads made the mistake of dropping to one knee, staying close to the building, unaware of the window above him. Of course, the enemy couldn't miss an opportunity like this so out of the window poured this bucket of shit and piss that was used for the party toilet all over the poor marine. Needless to say, that mistake never happened again.

After all the training and back at 42 Commando's base, we were out early morning standing to, awaiting an inspection from our commanding officer. On his inspection he stood behind me and he leaned forward and whispered in my ear: Come see me after the parade. I guessed he didn't need a response, so I stood silent and still, but my mind was wondering why? You can't help but think what have I done wrong. After the dismissal I made my way to his office. As I walked in, he said, No need to salute, have a seat – and gestured towards a chair. I want you in my Int team, he said. The Int team is the intelligence gathering section that, as it depicts, collates intelligence on the area which in turn is fed to the troops on the ground. It is largely done undercover, and you are not in uniform plus you could grow your hair long. You are deployed ahead of the company, so you have some knowledge of the ground before the rest of the company arrives. You will be going to Templer Barracks, Ashford, Kent on Monday morning for your training and clearance. You will be representing the unit so be on your best behaviour. That will be all, enjoy your course.

Talk about giving me time. Two days to prep. I knew exactly what was meant by that comment, a Royal Marine with his Green beret in an army camp always attracted attention, mostly good but there is always one who fancies the challenge to take you on. That was his way of saying do not rise to the bait or else. Remembering my unarmed combat lesson from my colour sergeant last time I made a mistake, ensured I would not make another, or at least not get caught.

This was somewhat unexpected and although exciting still sent a shiver down my spine. The Int training was very informative and although most of it I probably wouldn't use, it was another string to my bow of skills. The course I was sent on was largely used for undercover operations. The challenges of life as an undercover operative mean excellent observational ability, stamina and the ability to think under stress are all vital for undercover surveillance work. Since many operations require the operative to work alone, a sense of self-confidence and self-reliance is also a prerequisite. I was trained in advanced driving, including sustained high-speed driving, using a vehicle as a weapon, controlled crashes, skid recovery and anti-ambush skills. The demanding disciplines of surveillance – from hiding in ditches or attics, to following on foot, to surveillance from vehicles – were all taught. The ability to observe, follow and communicate over the radio network, all covertly, were taught to me. We were even taught how to break into houses, lock picking skills, more unarmed combat and small weapons handling. For me the weapon given as my personal weapon was the Browning 9mm. Unfortunately, nothing like the "do you feel lucky" 44 Magnum that Dirty Harry would carry. That said, I guess walking around Crossmaglen, Northern Ireland in a cowboy hat with a 44 Magnum is not so covert. So, I had to make do.

The difference in this training to my Arctic training was that this time it was for active service and very much close quarters. This gave you that tingle of mixed excitement and reality. What if. That said, my first deployment in Northern Ireland whilst filled with lots of scary tasks also had its humorous ones. I remember our deployment to the Maze prison or as some know it as the H blocks. The Maze prison was famous for being home to Bobby Sands, the first member of the IRA to die whilst being on hunger strike. I was stood at the entrance gate talking to the army guard just making small talk when the dustbin lorry approached the gate to leave. As it pulled up to the guard post, and once the hiss of the brakes had stopped, I thought I heard some screaming in the back of the truck. The guard and I looked at each other and slowly made our way to the driver's window. Would you mind just switching the engine off, I asked. Sure, came the reply and sure enough once the cab was silent the screams from the rear were unmistakable. Two crazy prisoners had somehow hidden in the bins and were consequently being crushed in the machine. They had made a valiant attempt of escape but failed to realise that the dustbin lorry actually crushed the rubbish and not just cart it. Sadly, one of the prisoners did not survive.

My time in Lisburn was eventful; being part of the Int team I had the freedom of not wearing uniform and the ability to drive around in a plain vehicle for my surveillance work. I recall popping into Lisburn Barracks, which is HQ Northern Ireland, one time to change the videos for the QRF team. QRF stands for quick reaction force. This is a small team who are basically sat around dressed to kill, waiting for an incident. So, they usually just watch movies or sleep. Each section on deployment takes it in turns to be QRF. Whilst I was in the video shop within the barracks, I overheard a couple of guys talking. One said to the other, you can't go down there as there are too many pigs around. The Humber Pig is a lightly armoured truck used by the British Army from the 1950s until the early 1990s. The Pig saw service with the Royal Ulster Constabulary (RUC) chiefly as an armoured personnel carrier from late 1958 until early 1970. This caught my attention so when I got back to the Maze I went into the office and onto the computer. Being on the Int team you have a high clearance on security and are able to check currently gathered intelligence reports. When looking at mugshots of people in the area who are suspected terrorists, who should come up but the lady who served me at the video shop. Interesting. I brought this to the attention of my boss who in turn brought it to the attention of the local permanent commander. Although she was not a suspected terrorist, what is not common knowledge is that anyone visiting the Maze prison is covertly photographed and a record kept for information. At the time the Maze prison was experiencing A class drugs finding their way in. The question now was why is a lady working in HQ Northern Ireland visiting the Maze prison. After much discussion it was decided I was to cajole her into trusting me to gain as much information as to why she is visiting the prison and working in HQ. The RUC special branch (Royal Ulster Constabulary) were also involved in the investigation on A class drugs getting into the Maze. What an interesting little job to land. A little outside my remit, but if we can help, we will. She was a good-looking girl, so my challenge was on. The next time I went into the video shop I struck up a conversation with her. I started to frequent the place more often. She asked me once what I was doing in Northern Ireland. I explained I was a civilian responsible for the entertainment equipment of the troops in the Maze, organising their entertainment, Christmas parties etc. Hence getting the videos sorted out. This gave me the cover to have access to military areas but as a civilian. She was writing a letter one time when I was visiting, and I said to her, Why don't you give me your mail to save you a stamp as I'm in and out every day. She agreed and in her first letter she had written, my postman is here, and time dated it, asking for a time date it was received. Little did she know her letters were opened, photocopied, sealed and delivered quicker than the normal post, giving us a build-up of who she was. I remember visiting her home on occasions, it was a scary drive as I had to cross a small bridge over a stream, and I used to imagine being compromised as military and the bridge blowing me sky high. I used to tense up every time I crossed it. Another scary moment was being sat in her lounge and the doorbell rang; two large Irish boys came into the kitchen and a conversation was being held obviously not for my ears. One of the lads poked his head into the lounge and said hello in a strong Irish accent. I just smiled and nodded, not wanting to let out my English accent, knowing how much we were hated at that time. This was during a time when knee capping and tar and feathering was prevalent.

It turned out she used to be married to an English squaddie (army personnel) which is how she was working in HQ Northern Ireland; she ended up getting divorced, but it was not common knowledge in HQ and she was now seeing a drug trafficker who was doing time in the Maze prison. She was still carrying out his business while he was inside. Once I left Northern Ireland she was lifted, and I received a nice thank you letter from the Maze commander. That was a fun job.

I had a number of interesting encounters in Northern Ireland during my time in the Corps and some very close shaves where I was lucky and thankful to get out unharmed. But this is an autobiography of some of my interesting experiences, not so much a war story.

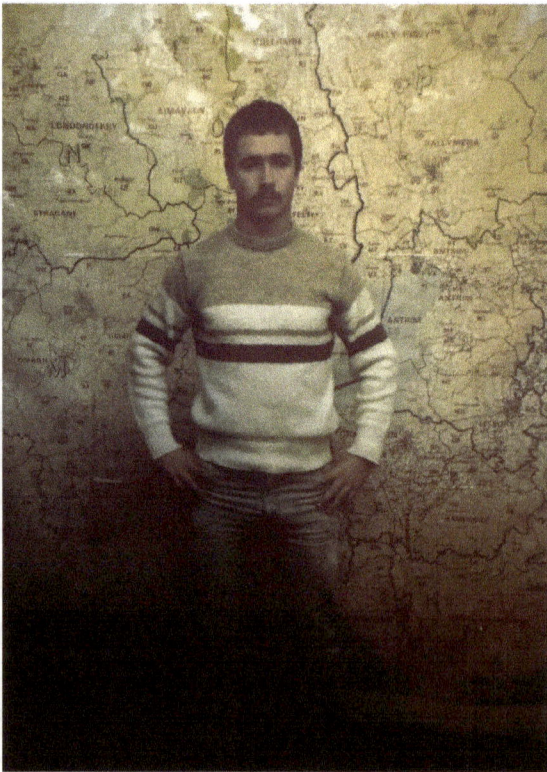

Figure 19 Giving a patrol an area brief Northen Ireland

Figure 20 Northern Ireland Maze Prison working undercover.

After my last tour in Northern Ireland, I returned to Spalding in Lincolnshire where my mother lived for a few weeks' R&R (Rest and Recuperation). I had visited my mother on many occasions and had good friends in Spalding. One in particular was an ex-Navy chap who now owned the Red Lion hotel in the town centre. I recall on my trip back to the town centre from the train station I called in at the Red Lion to say hello to my friend. Mistake number one as he was so glad to see me, he insisted I stayed for a few pints. The Red Lion used to have a bar and a lounge. The lounge you were not allowed in unless you had a shirt collar and tie on – except myself obviously, I was allowed in there any time being in favour of an ex-matelot (Sailor) they can't help themselves, they love to be around us bootnecks. I think it was about 2 am when I left the place a little worse for wear, I still had my Bergen backpack to carry home having come straight from Ireland. It was still quite a distance to my mother's house, so I decided to take a shortcut which took me behind the cinema and across the car park towards where my mother lived. Whilst I was walking across the car park, I came across a car I recognised; it belonged to my girlfriend at the time, Diane was her name. This was strange. What was her car doing in the car park behind the cinema? I walked towards it only to find her and another chap inside. I knocked on the window and to my surprise – or more to her surprise – the door was opened, and they were both inside enjoying themselves. Hello Diane, I said, what's going on here? I was promptly told to shut up and mind my own business by the person she was with. I ignored him for a little while and continued talking to Diane. Why don't you just fuck off? Came a voice from within; you're no longer wanted here. I think I told you to shut up, was my reply. I'm not currently talking with you. Having just come back from a hard tour in Northern Ireland and been to the pub with my friend, now worse for wear I was not in the mood for an idiot like him. Right, he said, making a move towards the door. I'm not quite sure what my thoughts were, but at this time I had the door open, one arm on the roof, the other on the door top. I pulled myself up, swung my foot in and kicked him. But the second I had done it I knew I shouldn't have, so I slammed the door and went on my way. I hadn't been walking long when a car happened to start coming down the road. I had a feeling this was a police car, being a little drunk and having done what I'd done. I didn't want to be caught by the police at this time of the night, so I faded with the shadows into the background and let the car go past. After it was some way down the road I stood up and carried on walking. It wasn't long before I noticed the car turn around and head back towards me; this time I just carried on walking. The police car then pulled up beside me and when I looked inside, I recognised one of the guys who I actually knew quite well. Hi Allen, he said, I guess you know why we're here. Yes, I replied, unfortunately I do. Come on, jump in and I'll give you a lift back to your mum's. En route home he explained to me if the guy makes a complaint they might have to come and speak with me tomorrow. Not a problem, I said, you know where I am. They were both sympathetic, understanding exactly what had happened but nevertheless I shouldn't have done it. The following morning, I got up early and decided to go out for an early morning run. I had a small backpack on and some Ronhill tracksuit bottoms. When returning to my house I noticed a police car parked on the drive outside the house. When I entered, there were two policemen having a cup of tea with my mother. Hello Allen, I guess you know why we're here. I didn't know these two, but they had obviously been briefed on me. I'm afraid we need you to come down to the station and make a statement. With that they thanked my mother, and I jumped in the police car and headed for the station. It was quite amusing when we got to the station as they had to put me in cells and prior to going in the cells they asked me to remove my laces from my trainers and the lace from around my waist holding up my Ronhills. The sergeant at the station who I knew laughed and said, hey guys this is a marine, he's not going to hang himself over a fight. So, I was allowed in the waiting cell without removing my laces. I made my statement then waited for the outcome. Unfortunately, my kick had lacerated the guy's face, and he had 13 stitches, albeit very small, it was still a bad situation to be in. Also, another stroke of bad luck was that his father was a solicitor. It was a couple of weeks before a court hearing but fortunately for me the court date was inconvenient for the lad's father to attend so the hearing was conducted between the two of us. Another positive for me, Captain Guyer, whom I had worked with as my boss on many occasions, came to the court hearing to testify to my character. I turned up very smartly dressed and stood in silence as the crime was read out. My boss then gave a statement to the court which even I was impressed with. Explaining the hard tour I had just returned home from and how totally out of character this was. The judge, being a woman, which I now believe helped, listened to both sides then asked if I had anything to say. I stood up and apologised to the court for the inconvenience I had caused and expressed my regret and assurance that it would never happen again. After a short deliberation I was fined £50 and bound over to keep the peace for 12 months. What a surprise: I thought I was going to be charged with Grievous bodily harm (GBH) and that would not have done my career any good. That evening, I had gotten my boss a room in the Red Lion Hotel and we were enjoying lots of drinks, also joined by the policemen who had arrested me. However, that was not the end of the matter. On my return to base camp, I was hauled in front of my commanding officer for bringing the Corps into disrepute. I was marched into my disciplinary hearing by none other than Mac, my troop sergeant, again. The Co had a copy of the Spalding Gazette in front of him with the front-page headline reading Marine hits rival. Oh shit. I was dressed down by my Co but not too harshly, I think there was a deep understanding of the situation but nevertheless I should have known better. No unarmed combat training this time, just a few extra duties. As we marched out of the office and the door closed, Mac turned to me and said, for fuck's sake, Allen, I would have done the same myself but what have I told you about getting caught? Will you ever learn. Don't get caught!

* * *

CHAPTER 6

J ungle warfare Training: Belize, Brunei or Malaysia are the
normal places where jungle warfare is carried out. But no, not
this time, this time we are going to Canada. Am I just born lucky
or what? I know I was born on Christmas Day, but really, not only
are we going to learn how to survive and fight in a hot humid
environment, but we are going to throw in some additional hazards
like bears. Yep, how lucky am I.

There can be few fighting environments that are more austere,
challenging and unforgiving than the jungle. The humidity, the
heat, the insects, everything works against you. As one of the
toughest environments you can find yourself operating in, there is
no place for failure. You simply have to survive. Experiences during
the Burma campaign and subsequent campaigns in Malaya and
Borneo during the Second World War taught us many lessons, and
it is no surprise that many of the world's elite Special Forces include
a jungle phase in their training to this day. Finding and fighting
the enemy in the jungle requires specialised jungle warfare skills
that UK Armed Forces personnel still practise on training exercises
in the tropical jungles. It is often said that if you can operate for
extended periods in the jungle, you will find other challenging
environments easy. Mmm, I kind of agree with that statement. I
must admit I hated my time in jungle training and would take the

Arctic over the jungle anytime. At least when you're cold you can get warm. But when you're hot how can you cool down? I won't bore you with the fine detail of jungle warfare, but I will give you my lessons learned.

Drink water, plenty of it! Hot and humid conditions in the jungle pose one of the greatest threats in the form of heat illness so it is crucial to drink water as often as possible and this should be sterilised to ensure that it is safe to drink. Choosing shelter wisely. Heavy rain in the jungle can lead to flash flooding so choosing where to assemble a shelter is vital – it should never be positioned next to a creek or stream. An enemy behind every rock. The threats from flora and fauna are constant in the jungle with mosquitos, sand-flies, spiders, scorpions, snakes, crocodiles and wildcats; and just to make it interesting in Canada we have bears too, as well as tree sap that can blind you and frogs that will make your skin burn. It is vital to respect these threats by leaving them well alone. I recall one evening as we stopped and set up camp, we were cooking and what should happen to come by with all the interesting smells. Yep Yogi himself, only he didn't look as friendly as the one I was used to. These things are huge. Prior to coming over to Canada we were informed how to act when confronted with a bear. If the bear is stationary, move away slowly and sideways; this allows you to keep an eye on the bear and avoid tripping. Moving sideways is also non-threatening to bears. Do NOT run, but if the bear follows, stop and hold your ground. Well that all went out the window, everyone just grouped up and yelled at the top of our voices. I think the noise and the size of the group intimidated the beast and it turned around and casually walked away. Needless to say, that night I slept with one eye open.

Prepare for the worst: the undergrowth of the jungle is too thick to use wheeled or tracked vehicles. So, movement is conducted by foot, and you often have to use machetes to cut through the thick vegetation. All movement becomes greatly slowed down due to the combination of mud, the thickness of jungle and extreme temperatures; covering just a short distance takes hours.

Stay green and keep quiet. Understanding the challenges this environment poses are essential when operating against and tracking a determined enemy, whilst simultaneously making it as difficult as possible to be tracked and attacked. Camouflage cream, or cam cream as it's known in the trade, should be worn at all times to blend into the green landscape and it is important to keep all noise to a minimum. You must stay aware. The thickness of the jungle floor's vegetation means that it is difficult for personnel to see each other, making it especially difficult to coordinate movement and directing fire on targets that are likely to be hidden by thick foliage. So, you must keep your eyes peeled. Weapons, which in other circumstances can fire accurately for hundreds of metres, are much less useful when constrained to only seeing a few metres. When operating in mountainous areas of the jungle, visibility is restricted by frequent mist and heavy rain. Unlike the mountains, Arctic or urban warfare jungle has its own set of demands; hygiene is one of them. The heat and sweat can quickly turn a cut or graze into a sore septic mess. It is easily done with equipment rubbing and the dirt and sweat opening your pores. You cannot underestimate the importance of hygiene and checking yourself on breaks.

Our visit to Canada for this type of training was another great experience. I recall the journey by bus from the airport to our destination. We were literally in the middle of nowhere when out of the blue a flashing police car pulled us over. Unsure why or what we had done, I waited to see what was afoot. This large Mountie boarded the bus. He was as most movies depict a Canadian Mountie with the exact same uniform. Royal Marines, he said, I'm here to warn you of some dangerous black bears roaming your area of destination. But fear not as two of them have no teeth and they are well known in this area as gummy bears. Ha bloody ha. With this, Mac our troop sergeant stood up and embraced the man he was good friends with and was himself an ex bootneck, so we had a police escort for the rest of our journey and Mac rode in the police car.

So far in my career on every trip something funny has happened to me and Canada was no exception. After our training and exercise we got a little bit of R&R time before returning back to the UK. On this particular night we went out to a club. Prior to going to the club, we visited a bar and the strange thing about the bars in Canada, you were not allowed to lift your pint and move it from one table to the other. You had to get the waitress to move the drink whilst you moved to the table you wanted. Anyway, after the pub we went to a club. A good night was had by all, time to let off a little steam. When the club closed, we headed for food, the local kebab shop for your greasy kebab and chips to soak up the alcohol. Whilst sitting eating and having a crack with the lads, a police car turned up and parked outside, the policeman was busy eyeballing us and eventually came into the kebab shop. He walked over to me and asked me if I would accompany him to his police car as he had received a complaint about me. About me? I asked, but I did nothing. I replied, holding my hands up. With this the guys all started saying it wasn't him it was me, officer, a bit like the movie 'I am Spartacus'. As you can imagine a dozen guys all dressed the same with moustaches, it was difficult to identify who was who. Anyway, as instructed I accompanied him to his police car and once in his car, he said I had been accused of assaulting somebody. This was news to me as I had simply had a good night and don't recall any conflict at all. He explained we would have to go to the police station to write a statement and be identified by the accuser. This was not a problem for me as I had done nothing, so I was clearly misidentified. Once at the police station I was put into a small room with a one-way window. The accuser is at the other side of the window. I had to face left, face right and look straight forward just like being photographed for a criminal record. When the officer returned to the room, he confirmed that I had been identified as the person who committed the crime. I was still unaware of what the crime was, so I asked the officer what exactly it is I am being accused of. You're being accused of sexual assault, he said. Oh my God, sexual assault is a serious crime in the UK. I am definitely not the person she thinks I am. Surely if she has been assaulted there will be marks on her and some sort of forensic evidence could be available. No, he said, she has no marks as there was no physical contact. No physical contact? I said. Then how has she been sexually assaulted? With this the officer got down on his knees and proceeded to hold his hands up beside his face and stuck his tongue out, wiggling it up and down. It took all of my resolve not to laugh, it was like something out of a comic book. So this action in Canada is classed as sexual assault. How bizarre, but still it was not me, I made no such actions. This line of questioning went on for hours and it was already the early hours of the morning. Eventually the police officer came back into my room and explained that the boyfriend was the one who had made the complaint and that in fact he could not positively identify me and that the accusation was to be retracted. He apologised to me for the inconvenience and proceeded to offer me a lift back to my base camp. As we arrived at our campsite, Mac, our Troop Sergeant, was up and about and came over to talk to the officer. When the officer left. Mac came over to me and said are you just a magnet for trouble, Wood? It seems to follow you wherever you go! I laughed, I guess I must have one of those faces that everyone loves. Get your head down, take an hour's rest and we move out in three hours. Thank God for that, back to the good old UK and out of this horrible jungle.

* * *

CHAPTER 7

T here comes a time in your career as a Royal Marine Commando and being under the Navy's umbrella that you will have to spend some time on board one of her Majesty's ships, no matter how much ducking and diving you do to avoid it, you will at one time, or another serve on board.

Every day we have DROs (daily routine orders) posted on a noticeboard. Often on this noticeboard any special operations or courses are highlighted, and you can apply. On this particular day they were looking for marines to serve time on Her Majesty's Endurance.

HMS *Endurance* was a Chatham-based Royal Navy ice patrol ship deployed in the Southwestern Atlantic. Her primary role was to maintain a British presence in the Antarctic area and to provide support for the Overseas British Territory of the Falklands. The ship would spend each Antarctic summer in the southern hemisphere, conducting hydrographic and oceanographic surveys, acting as support ship for the British Antarctic Survey and Guard ship. The ship was originally the Danish vessel *Anita Dan*, built by Krogerwerft, Rendsburg, launched in May 1956. The *Anita Dan* was purchased from Denmark in 1967. In 1968 the ship was converted for Royal Navy use. During the conversion the hull was strengthened for operations in the ice, scientific and surveying equipment was installed as well as the addition of a flight deck and hanger for two Royal Navy Wasp helicopters. An unusual feature for a RN ship was that her hull and mast were painted vivid red for easy identification in the ice; the ship was affectionately known as the 'Red Plum'. She was 305ft long x 46ft wide and had a maximum displacement of 3600 tons. The ship's complement was 119 (13 officers and 106 ratings, including a small detachment of Royal Marines) plus 12 spare berths for scientists. During the Falklands conflict, *Endurance* was commanded by Captain Nick Barker and carried 22 Royal Marines. She was a major Signals Intelligence asset. Her helicopters helped disable the Argentine submarine *Santa Fe* and launch the final assault that recaptured South Georgia. The final enemy surrender off the South Sandwich Islands was signed in her wardroom. She also rescued two wildlife filmmakers caught up in the conflict. To be able to serve on her you have to be Arctic trained. Most of you may recognise HMS Endurance from the start of the Falklands war, the famous newspaper headline about "When 22 British Marines Held off a Superior Argentine Invasion Force & a Naval Corvette". The 22 men aboard her were the detachment of marines that held off the Argentinian attack for quite some time before eventually surrendering and being returned to the UK. Many of whom returned to the Falklands conflict to continue the fight.

My time had come – if I did not apply for this position, I might end up being on a grey ship, which is a completely different arena. So, the thought of becoming part of the 13-strong marine detachment interested me. Particularly as it was Arctic-bound, Endurance's job was to map uncharted waters in the Antarctic. The Marines' job on board was firstly to defend the ship if required but also to look after the British Antarctic survey team aboard her. My application was successful, and it wasn't long before I was given my marching orders to start preparation for boarding.

So here we go again, another canvas, another bout of learning, another string to the bow. We were shipped off to HMS Raleigh, located near Torpoint in Cornwall. HMS Raleigh is the largest Royal Navy training establishment in the Southwest (set across a 239-acre site) and is the front door to a career in the Royal Navy; however, we were there for our induction to life onboard a ship. "Yawn," I hear you say. But to be fair it was in fact an eye opener for us as well as a refresher of other skills. The School of Maritime Survival provides Royal Navy personnel with vital skills in firefighting, damage control and first aid to maintain safety. All sailors must undergo this training before taking up an appointment at sea and we were no different; although we were the Navy's Soldiers, our time spent on a ship is very limited and because we were now becoming part of a ship's detachment, we also had to undertake orientation and training of life on board. Our training here was fun. HMS Raleigh has a number of first-class facilities and purpose-built simulators. Of course, being Royal Marines in a naval training establishment there was no holds barred. Our training was certainly not softly softly; in fact, quite the opposite as the Matelots would love to try to crack us. But as we say, "I'm a rubber duck and you won't quack me".

I remember the fun we had in the damage control section of the simulator. This is a simulator constructed like a ship's hull, and it has various shaped holes in the sides and at the bottom; you are locked into the simulator and a timer is put on before they open the floodgates. Water is then pouring into the cubicle, and you have been left various shaped wedges and hammers to try and limit the water coming in. This type of damage control obviously has to be done quickly as the more water comes in the more chance the ship sinks; however, the navy boys thinking it was funny decided not to give us enough wedges so there was little or no chance of stopping the water coming in, particularly as we were under pressure of time. Once the water reaches a set level in a given time you have failed.

If you can stem the water and delay the level till the time limit is reached you pass. On the observation deck there are a number of Wrens as well as sailors watching the exercise. Our nickname for sailors is Jolly Jack and what Jolly Jack didn't anticipate is that failure is not an option, more so when up against competition. It quickly became apparent to us what was going on when we noticed we had run out of wedges. Jolly Jack failed to understand that Marines adapt very quickly as they go so the obvious thing was to strip down and use our shoes and clothing to block the holes. Much to the amusement of all the Wrens watching, you are now left with a bunch of naked Marines having used every possible item to stem the flow of water, that left very little water coming into the compartment. Needless to say, we passed but news had quickly spread round the base of what had happened, which attracted a lot of attention when we entered the galley for lunch. But hey, who doesn't like attention?

We spent three weeks in Raleigh being taught various skills and terminology. Rudder, anchor, bow, keel, accommodation, propeller, mast, bridge, hatch coves and bow thrusters are some common visible parts. In contrast, bulkheads, frames, cargo holds, hopper tank, double bottom, girders, cofferdams, side shell etc., are the invisible parts of a ship. The most forward part of a ship is called a Bow; the left-hand side of the ship is referred to as port, whereas the right side is called starboard. Likewise, the front side is termed as forward and the backside as astern. The Navy has their own language. As well as being taught confined firefighting skills and using the breathing apparatus, how to enter and leave port is also important to ensure safe passage. When entering a harbour or river mouth, lateral buoy markers are used to map out a safe route through the water. Upon entry the red can-shaped port buoys should remain on a driver's left-hand side, whilst the green starboard buoys should be on the right. Upon exit this rule is naturally reversed.

There was a lot of enjoyable lessons but I think the guys enjoyed the various types of knots the Navy use, not too dissimilar to our mountain rescue knots; it did give the opportunity for payback as Naval personnel were frequently found secured to the occasional flag post or strapped to one of the Wrens' bed post for when she returned to her accommodation. Such fun.

Thankfully part of our ship's training landed us back with our own kind as we did five days with the raiding squadron. RM Tamar is a special place where 1 Assault Group Royal Marines live. It's also home to 539 Assault Squadron and 10 (Landing Craft) Training Squadron. Made up of more than 100 personnel, 539 Assault Squadron is equipped with a range of high-tech landing craft, including Rigid Raiders, the Griffon 2000TD hovercraft, and the Viking amphibious armoured vehicle, which is used to deliver troops to land. The squadron has carried out operations in Iraq and Somalia and contributed to security at the London 2012 Olympics. The unit is named after the famed 539 Assault Flotilla, which played a crucial role in the Normandy Landings. Here we enjoyed racing up and down the Tamar in rigid raiders and generally enjoying some fun time away from the Navy barracks we were assigned to. Of course, we were being taught maritime skills as well. It wasn't all just play time.

After our induction to the Navy ways and terminology we were sent to Portsmouth. Because I was already a dive instructor, I was assigned to be in charge of the ship's diving. But first I had to do a specialist diving course with the Navy.

The Defence Diving School is a Joint Service Training Establishment providing military diving training to both Royal Navy and Army personnel. All Navy clearance divers and Army divers carry out their basic training at the school's headquarters on Horsea Island on the north shore of Portsmouth Harbour. Myself and one other marine were sent on this course. Yet again we were being plunged into an environment whereby because we were Royal Marine Commandos we were perceived as superhumans, so everything had to be made difficult for us, and any examples it was always the two of us to demonstrate. It does get rather tedious at times. But then again c'est la vie. I'm a rubber duck and you can't quack me.

The course I was assigned to was a little bit special. It wasn't just a ship's diver course, nor was it a clearance diver course, it lay just in between. As well as the Navy's Way of diving we were taught underwater welding and cutting techniques; most of this was due to the type of ship I was deployed on – Endurance was always as far south as the Navy has ever been so quite isolated. As a result, it needed to be self-sufficient and prepared for any eventuality. Being physically fit is obviously a skill required for underwater diving; physical challenges are always fun for Royal Marines, but I will say that the log runs when the tide is out were a hell of a challenge. More so when you were up against the Navy and army divers and being expected to lead the way, you would have one log between two and the log was almost half a tree, you had a 200 metre run to do from the beach head to the water, then you would get waist high in the water, turn around and run back, all this whilst being enclosed in a dry suit. The chief petty officer in charge of our training for some reason took a shine to me and I could tell he was hoping to find some way to fail me. One time I was getting ready to do a navigation dive, I was standing at the water's edge helping my oppo (oppo being the term used for friend) when the chief petty officer walked by; as he passed me, he barged me into the water. Where we entered the water, it was a straight drop from the side into approximately 10 metres' depth of water. The zip on a Navy dry suit is at the rear of the suit between the shoulder blades. Once dressed your oppo usually completes the dry suit by zipping up for you. The chief petty officer was well aware that my dry suit was not yet zipped as he pushed me into the water. Consequently, my suit started to fill with water. Two of the other divers rushed forward to help me. Stand back! shouted the chief petty officer. Lesson one: do not stand too close to the water's edge until you are fully suited. I reached forward to hold onto the edge of the harbour wall. Stay back from the wall, he shouted at me. Tread water. Treading water in a dry suit is easy provided it's sealed, and you have a little air in there but mine was very quickly filling up and the more water that entered the heavier I got and the harder it was to keep my head above water. However, this did not deter him from making me suffer. I continued to tread water while he continued to go on about how dangerous it is to stand too close to the water with an open dry suit. It wasn't long before my dry suit was totally full and I was struggling to stay afloat; however, I was not going to let him win. After what felt like an eternity, he allowed me to get to the edge and hold on, but would not allow any of the others to help me out of the water. For the rest of that day's diving I was left wet and cold. There were many times during that day I wished there was nobody around apart from me and him and I could give him some lessons on unarmed combat.

All said and done, the course was a good one and I was fortunate enough to do some training with our SBS (Special Boat Service) colleagues on their rebreathers and some night navigation exercises. Rebreather diving is underwater diving using diving rebreathers, a class of underwater breathing apparatus which recirculate the breathing gas exhaled by the diver after replacing the oxygen used and removing the carbon dioxide metabolic product. Rebreather diving is practised by recreational, military and scientific divers in applications where it has advantages over open circuit scuba, and surface supply of breathing gas is impracticable. The main advantages of rebreather diving are extended gas endurance, low noise levels, and lack of bubbles. Which is why it is favoured by the SBS.

During the course we did some deep dives where we would end up in decompression chambers. Decompression chambers, also known as hyperbaric chambers, simulate the atmospheric conditions that divers experience underwater. These chambers allow divers to gradually decompress and safely return to the surface without experiencing DCS (Decompression Sickness). Decompression chambers work by increasing the pressure of the environment around the diver. This allows the diver to off-gas the nitrogen and other gases absorbed while diving slowly. By gradually reducing the pressure, the nitrogen in the bloodstream can be safely eliminated, reducing the risk of DCS, or as commonly referred to, the bends. Singing was the traits of the day whilst in the chamber because you all sound like Mickey Mouse with the high pitched voice.

Another job which was my responsibility on board was rescue diver and in my preparation for this, we did a lot of high jumps and jumping out of helicopters into the water to rescue others. The finale of the course as well as examinations was a final exercise which involved a lot of what we had just been taught and finished on a night navigation dive. On the last day of the course and the night before the final examination day, the chief petty officer came to see me. Allen, he said, I think I ought to take you out for a few drinks as a way of saying congratulations for not cracking despite me pushing you to the limits. No thanks, I said, I'd like to rest up ready for tomorrow's exercise. No no, come on, I insist. I'll pick you up at 8 o'clock, be ready. That's an order. I knew what his game was. He was going to try and get me wrecked as a final attempt to have me fail, but if there's one thing I'm renowned for that's holding my drink. So, I agreed to go out with him in the knowledge it would be him that gets wrecked.

Sure enough that evening he was plying me with drinks so I decided we would go onto whisky chasers, whisky being my favourite tipple. It wasn't long before his speech was slurring, and his legs were having trouble keeping him up. He took me to a club called Joanna's which was a sticky carpet typical navy nightclub. One I was to visit again in the not-too-distant future. Around 1 am, I said I was going to leave and go back to the barracks because we were up at 06:30. He still hadn't given up and insisted that I come home and have a few drinks at his house, so we got a taxi to his place. When we got to the door, his wife was not overly impressed. She opened the door dressed in a sheer baby doll nightdress and was a little surprised to see me holding up her husband. He insisted I come in. I could see the look on her face of horror as she thought oh no. He introduced me as one of the Marines on his course. Anyway, once we got in the door, he staggered off to the toilet and that was the last I saw of him. I made some small talk with his wife and apologised about his state. She was very flirtatious with me and I was half tempted. That would've been a real payback, but I thought better of it. Made my excuses and got a taxi back to the barracks. The following morning, I was up bright and breezy and what a surprise he was slightly late and when he arrived, he apologised to the group. I could see it in his face. He was not impressed. His final attempt to try and make me fail did not succeed. I completed the course then headed back to base. Happy to see the likes of him behind me.

It was good to reunite with my colleagues who were now going to be the guys I spend the next 18 months on board a ship with. It was time for some social bonding as a team. The Navy boxing championship was being held during that week and we enjoyed going to watch the bouts. We had a good week together, plenty of sports, out to the pubs, bit of shopping, find out what we needed to take with us on the trip and finally Saturday night on our rounds checking out all the local pubs. I was explaining to the guys about the Chief Petty Officer and what an ass he was and it was decided that we would check out this club, Joanna's, that I mentioned previously. It was a rough nightclub, but full of girls and I don't mean the Matelots. And fairly close by.

When we arrived, it was jam packed with all the navy boys, most of the boxing squad including the Navy boxing champion who had just won the competition. We stood in a circle as a group. I guess we stood out a bit as obviously being marines. All of us were sporting a moustache, which was the style at the time. I guess we did look a bit intimidating as a group of marines amongst all these navy boys. It wasn't long before the boxing champion, who had had a few drinks, decided he wanted to throw some challenges our way, he came over to our group and was making a bit of an ass of himself. He picked on the biggest guy with us, Tony, a big Northern Marine who brushed him off with his hand and said go away, little man. The boxing champion being coaxed by his colleagues decided to go round all of us one by one, asking us if we would step outside with him eventually making his way back round to Tony. Right? Said Tony, Allen here, the smallest guy amongst us, will take you outside and teach you a lesson whilst we get him his next round. Oh shit, I couldn't exactly say no and lose face, but it wasn't something I particularly relished doing. Mine is a bottle of Becks, I said, come on then, let's get this over with. I was very nervous as I was walking down the steep stairs to the entrance of the club – after all, this guy had just won the Navy championship at boxing. I stopped at the entrance and spoke to the bouncer. Will it be okay to come back in once we've sorted this out? I asked. Yes Royal, he said, thank you for taking it outside. As we walked around the corner from the club, I turned around to face the guy and then just launched myself at him. Fortunately, there was a small garden wall about knee high which when I launched at him, he fell over with me landing on top of him, immediately he put his hands up and said okay okay, no trouble intended. Phew, to me that was a lucky escape. When I stood up to walk back to the club the boys had followed me out and were waiting at the corner watching to see what would happen. I guess also making sure no harm came to me. Time to move on, Tony said, sorry about that, Al, but thought it was quite amusing. Mmm, for you maybe, I replied. Bonding – isn't it fun.

All our courses now completed and our orientation to dos and don'ts aboard a Navy ship, it was time to join her. We left our barracks and headed to board our new floating accommodation for the next 18 months. We were shown below decks to our new mess deck. As expected down steep steps to the hull of the ship, opening a watertight door and being confronted by a fairly small, dull, very grey room – the space was designed for 15 guys including small lockers for each man; the bunk beds were three high. It was a depressing thought having to spend 18 months here. We spent the next two weeks getting oriented on the boat, understanding our role and making ourselves feel at home. One morning after coming back from our PT session, a bright red carpet had been delivered and was lying on the forward deck. Our ML (mountain leader), a guy called Des Finesse, said, guys, I think that's our new carpet, drag it down and let's get it fitted. Our old dull green and grey carpet was quickly ripped up and the bright new red carpet laid. Next was to re-decorate, being a red and white ship. The only paint we could find was red and white, so we mixed this together and hey presto we had a red carpet and pink lockers and walls. On the grey watertight door, we painted some jail bars as a window, so it looked like you were walking into a jail cell. It was starting to feel more like Home. I will always remember our clear lower decks. Clear lower decks is a term where you stand to and present your accommodation and the ship, ready for inspection for hygiene. This is a walk-through with the skipper, navigator and a couple of other officers. The look on their faces as they came into the marines' mess, I will never forget. Des being the senior member had to present the room. The skipper looked at him. Pink! Corporal Finesse? Yes, sir, he replied, we could only lay our hands on red or white paint, red being too aggressive and white being a little clinical. We thought a nice passive colour like pink would help keep the mood calm. I see, he said. Turning to the Navigator, he asked, Is this the red carpet that was delivered for the wardroom? Nobody said a word. Very well, carry on. We got away with it, but I think the skipper was just showing a gesture of goodwill for his marine detachment. The good thing about serving your time on a ship like Endurance is that it's not too military, we were given a fairly free rain. The skipper allowed the Marines to do their own thing, and our boss was also very relaxed. We didn't have to wear uniforms every day and when we did turn to, provided we were all dressed smart and the same it was allowed.

Time was passing and our setting sail on the journey to the South Atlantic was fast closing in. A final exercise before we left. HMS Endurance had to do a three-day sea trial test before setting sail. A sea trial is the testing phase of a watercraft (including boats, ships, and submarines). It is also referred to as a "shakedown cruise" by many naval personnel. It is usually the last phase of completion and takes place on open water, and it can last from a few hours to many days. The ship and its crew are put through their paces to ensure all is ready for the task ahead. This was mostly to do with the Navy side of things, so we had our own scenario test to conduct whilst the Navy boys were tested on theirs.

Our scenario was that the British embassy had been overrun and the Ambassador and his wife had been taken hostage and moved to a secret location. Because HMS Endurance was the closest vessel, the task was assigned to us. Our Intelligence had been given the location of the possible hideout. Our mission was to find and report back confirmation that the Ambassador and his wife were at the location and alive. After we had been given our task, we then prepared our plan of action. Our brief and action plan was done on a 3-D model of the ground we were entering; the hide was an old, listed farmhouse with three barn houses surrounding it. We were helicoptered onto Dartmoor at night and dropped off approximately five miles from the expected hide. I don't think I've ever had a night on Dartmoor that wasn't wet, misty and boggy; tonight was no exception. We were dropped off by Sea King helicopter and as we jumped from the helicopter to the deck onto the marshy ground of Dartmoor, we took up defensive positions and waited for the helicopter to be out of sight. The weather was typical of Dartmoor, horrible cold drizzle and damp soggy ground. We orientated ourselves and then headed off for the five mile yomp (Royal Marine Terminology for march or long trek) to our destination. Navigation in the black of night on Dartmoor is slow. Dartmoor is full of bogs which almost act like quicksand if you get stuck in them, so route selection has to be carefully thought out. About two hours later we arrived at our first RV. We radioed back to base that we were in our holding position. Now we would set up a base, get some camouflage shelter sorted out and prepare for the next stage. The farmhouse was about a kilometre further up. After a short break Tony and I were to move forward into an OP position (observation point). We prepared ourselves by getting into our ghillie suits. A ghillie suit is a type of camouflage clothing designed to resemble the background environment – such as foliage, sand or snow. In this case it was typically Dartmoor foliage, grass, moss and reeds. We made our way slowly towards the farmhouse and found ourselves a nice observation point, taking cover in a small, recessed gully. We had night vision binoculars and night vision scopes on our weapons. We put down a camouflage gortex insulator between the ground and our bodies just to prevent the cold, damp, wet Dartmoor ground seeping into our clothing. There is nothing worse than trying to lie perfectly still when you're freezing as it's very difficult to stop shivering. The insulated layer prevented this. The place was in darkness, no lights, no sign of vehicles. You could hear a pin drop. That seemed unusual. If it was a hide, you would generally have at least a guard and there would certainly be some light within the building; nevertheless, our job was to observe and report back. We took it in turns being watchmen and as dawn came about, we could see the muddy tracks leading up to the farmhouse but still no sign of movement or for that matter any vehicles. The farmhouse was a white listed building. The walls were covered in moss and in quite a bad state of repair, the windows looked single glazed and the doors typical old barn doors that opened from both the top and bottom. There were two main points of entry to the building according to our intelligence. One front door and one side door. We could see both from our position. There had been no movement apart from the occasional vermin or fox but nothing to log; we remained in position, quiet, still and observant. Dartmoor was still bleak, a gentle whistling wind in the background and the drizzle had still not gone away. We had been in position for some 12 hours now before we finally took sight of an old Land Rover making its way up the track towards the farmhouse followed by two black Range Rovers. They parked just outside the side entrance to the farmhouse. Four guys got out of the first vehicle and another four out of the last vehicle. Two guys opened the large double doors to the first outhouse. The guys from the rear vehicle seemed to be checking over the house. All were armed with AK-47 and M-16 assault rifles. We fed back descriptions to the head base and also to the rest of our troop waiting behind us. The driver and passenger of the middle range Rover got out of the vehicle and opened the rear doors. Finally, we had confirmation as they dragged out the ambassador and his wife from the rear seats. The three vehicles were then driven into the outhouse and the outhouse doors closed. Everyone was now within the farmhouse. We continued our observations, logging all movements, awaiting further instructions. Remain in position was the order. It wasn't long before smoke started to bellow out of the farmhouse chimney and I couldn't help but imagine them sat in front of a nice open fire, eating hot food whilst we were in the cold damp wet with nothing but a bag of nutty. Prior to going out on operations like this it is common to mix a bag of nuts, chocolate, Kendal mint bar and various other sweets and biscuits, put them all into a bag and smash it up. This is used as snacks to curb any hunger. It's known as a nutty bag. But boy what I would give right now for an open fire and hot drink. We lay and observed for another two hours whilst waiting for command headquarters to give us the next instruction. The kidnappers were clearly overconfident as they had not put outside sentries to alert for any incoming visitors, nor had they drawn any curtains over the windows, much to our advantage.

Although heavily armed, they were not too proficient, they had not separated the hostages but kept them in the same room. They were clearly not professional at this. My earpiece came to life with further instructions. Provided the ambassador and his wife were not being harmed and there were no signs of unrest we were to wait till dusk and then commence our rescue. This made perfect sense – the longer the kidnappers stayed in the hide the more confident they felt with their safety and waiting for dusk meant our exposure is limited as we advance to rescue. Perfect. We signalled the rest of the team to prepare for phase two, the rescue. Phase two meant Tony and myself would remain in our hide as a cut off group to help guide and cover the teams and prevent anyone escaping the building; the rest of the troop would split up into two four-man teams, each team taking the doors, one four-man team at the front door, one four-man team at the side door. Anyone choosing to escape through the windows would be taken down by ourselves. Dusk quickly arrived, everyone confirmed their readiness, smokes, thunder flashes, ammunition and everyone was 100% certain of their role.

We watched as team one approached the front door and simultaneously team two reached the side door. It was astonishing that nobody was even on lookout. Three, two, one: both doors breached, a loud bang as smoke and thunder flashes were sent into the room. Suddenly there were gunshots. We could observe the flash and bang from where we were lying. Screams and noise as the kidnappers panicked. The confirmation in my earpiece as rooms were being cleared. A loud smashing of glass echoed in the dusk night as one of the kidnappers tried to jump from the side window. Tony took a shot and as the kidnapper hit the floor, he lay their stationary. Everything seems to go in slow motion when your adrenaline is going in a situation like this yet it's all over in about five minutes. We had one 'dead' kidnapper, two 'badly injured' and seven secured, with the ambassador and his wife unharmed. A little shaken but nevertheless in good health. I called it in, and it wasn't long before we were surrounded by rescue services, ambulances, police, fire engines and lots of naval personnel. We quietly regrouped and made our way to the final RV where we were picked up by a Sea King helicopter and taken back to HMS Endurance. It was time to get warm, get some hot food down, clean up and get ready for our next adventure on one of her Majesty's ships.

Finally, we have finished all the preparations, training and familiarisation and we are ready to set sail on our 18-month detachment with HMS Endurance. We are prepared to be used anywhere we might be needed during our detachment, and we are equipped to defend the ship against any type of attack or takeover. First, we must sail to London to pick up the British Antarctic Survey team who will be joining us for the trip to the South Antarctic.

During our time in London, I had the opportunity to dive with the Metropolitan Police diving team; this was more by luck than anything else. Whilst being docked in London the officers had what we marines call a cock and arse party. It's when the officers have a party onboard the ship in the officers' mess. The guests, usually politicians and high dignitaries, come on board and enjoy being shown the ship. One of the guests was the chief of the Met diving team and he asked if he could look at our set up on board, obviously with me being in charge of this I was the one who showed him the works. It just so happened that the following day the Met police were due to dive in the Thames to recover a vehicle with a suspected body within and we were invited to join the dive. This was being filmed for TV by Thames TV and was a major news article. The following morning we met at the banks of the Thames, I was with my boss and one of the Navy navigators, the navigator being a senior officer was the one who had been invited to dive with the Met police. The problem with the Thames is you can't see anything in the water, it is murky and muddy so when doing a bottom search everybody is tied together and you enter the water like a daisy chain. Once everyone is in you then sink to the bottom and crawl along the bottom searching for what you're looking for, mostly by touch. I sat in the Met diving truck which holds all the equipment, chatting to the other diving guys who were there for maintenance and kit preparation. As the divers started to descend, the TV crews were filming for the news broadcast when suddenly they all surfaced again. The problem when being tied together is it's one up, all up. When they got back to the shoreline our Navy navigator was the one who brought them back up. He complained that there was an issue with the equipment. Obviously, this was becoming somewhat embarrassing, more so as the TV was doing the exposure on the dive. The equipment was brought to the dive truck to be inspected. It soon became apparent that there was nothing wrong with the equipment. Diving in the Thames can be quite claustrophobic and when the Met diving team asked me what my thoughts were, I could see nothing wrong with the equipment either, so I shrugged my shoulders, indicating that I guess he just got a bit panicky. With this the diving maintenance team explained there was nothing wrong with the equipment and suggested that I take the dive using the same equipment. So, it was fun for me. I got to dive in the Thames. We found the vehicle, strapped it up for the crane to lift out and I enjoyed a good drink with the team afterwards. When we were due to leave London, the divers I had been with presented me with a Metropolitan diving team plaque and a little thank you note for getting them out of an embarrassing situation. It was a good experience for me although I must admit diving in the Thames is not enjoyable.

Figure 21 Endurance entering London

Figure 22 Thames Dive London

Figure 23 Met Police Divers Unit

Finally, we had everyone on board, fully stocked and early the following morning we set sail for the South Atlantic.

* * *

CHAPTER 8

Our journey by sea from the United Kingdom to Stanley Harbour, Falkland Islands is about 8500 nautical miles. Our first stop was going to be Cadiz in Spain, but to get there we had to cross the Bay of Biscay which is known for its rough seas and violent storms and much of this is thanks to its exposure to the Atlantic Ocean. It is along the western coast of France from Brest, south to the Spanish border, and the northern coast of Spain west to Cape Ortegal. It was during this crossing that we hit our first problem. The weather came in bad and we were expecting a Force 12 storm. The skipper decided to anchor up and let the storm pass before we crossed the bay. Unfortunately, this didn't work out quite as expected and the storm was dragging us towards the land. A decision was made to lift anchor and head further out to sea to try and ride the storm. Unfortunately, when trying to lift the anchor, it was found to be snagged and after several failed attempts, the divers were called to investigate why the anchor could not be lifted. If we could ascertain how the anchor was snagged, we could direct the ship in a direction to unsnag it and then sail out to sea into the storm to prevent us being grounded. As you can imagine, with the waves smashing into the side of the boat it was an extremely dangerous and difficult task to get divers into the water. However, not getting the divers in the water could result in the ship being grounded, having been dragged towards the coast. It was therefore imperative we got in the water to decipher the ship's direction to free up the anchor. So once again it was down to the marines to get the job done. As I was the most experienced diver, I presumed I would be the one to dive with one other buddy. I was already kitted out and ready to get over when my boss Captain Guyer decided I would be better placed directing and tending the divers – at least then I could be ready should there be an issue. Obviously when diving in these conditions you had to be tied and your support was on the boat holding the rope so you could always be dragged back should there be a problem.

So, it was decided I was to attend to him. Fletch the other marine diver was already in the water being held by rope by another marine. In Captain Guyer's hurry to get into the water and away from the smashing waves, he jumped overboard without his fins on. It took all my strength to hold him steady as Tony lowered his fins to him tied to some rope, all the while trying to be discreet so as not to highlight his mistake – it would be the talk of the town had it been noticed. During all the commotion the anchor had somehow freed up and we got the divers back out of the water and headed out to sea, hoping for the best. I don't have the best sea legs as it is, but that crossing was one of the worst I've encountered, the ship was just like a cork bobbing around the waves. The navy boys, however, found it highly amusing. I think they nicknamed me Casper for a little while as I was as white as a ghost with a lifeless expression during the whole crossing.

Our trip to the South Atlantic and to the Falklands was quite good. Our first port of call was Cadiz in Spain. That was the first time we were allowed off ship and onto dry land. It was good to get onto dry land and stretch the legs. We were there for three days and we took every opportunity to exercise outside with early morning runs and physical circuits. One thing you do miss is open space training –

as you can imagine, running around the boat is extremely boring. Weight training on a ship is an art in itself – when doing bench press the ship bounces up and down with the waves, the weights tend to get light and heavy between waves so controlling the bench press is quite difficult. Life on board ship was quite interesting. For example, washing your clothes, we had a Chinese laundry, well, a laundry run by a Chinese man more to the point. You had to pay to have your laundry washed and dried, and you would hand in your washing bag each time you needed clean clothes. He was a civilian attached to the ship. I'm sure it was quite lucrative for him as he had a captive customer base. We also had a shop onboard where we could purchase essentials like shampoo, cigarettes, soap, razor blades and of course beer.

My time on HMS Endurance took me to quite a few places on the journey to and from the South Atlantic. I visited Cadiz, Madeira, Lisbon, Venezuela, Rio de Janeiro just to name a few. However, all the exciting adventures happened down south with the British Antarctic survey team. Port Stanley in the Falklands was our base. We would come back to Port Stanley every three to four weeks to restock before going back out to sea surveying in the Antarctic. Here was an opportunity to experience the haunting beauty and myriad wildlife of one of the most extreme climates of the world and to visit South Georgia, the South Sandwich Islands, the South Orkneys, the Graham Land Peninsula and Antarctica itself, areas first explored by men like Cook, Scott and Shackleton.

In the Defence Review of 1981, HMS Endurance was to have been withdrawn from the South Atlantic and scrapped. It is believed that this proposal more than any other single factor caused the Argentines to think that they could seize the Falklands, and hang onto them, without a fight. Incongruous though it might seem, Endurance, a tubby, bright-red freighter bought second-hand from the Danes in 1967, is the symbol of the British presence in the South Atlantic and Antarctic waters. Her duties are to act as the Falklands guardship, to support scientists of the British Antarctic Survey, and to survey uncharted waters for the Navy's Hydrographer.

Since 1982 her role as guardship has been taken over by the frigate and destroyer squadron deployed round the Falklands, and Endurance's duties are now almost exclusively in Antarctic waters and South Georgia.

The other main symbol of the British presence in the Antarctic is the British Antarctic Survey. Like Endurance, the Survey (always known as BAS) has had a change of fortune since the Falklands conflict, in the form of £15 million of extra funds to expand its activities. BAS has its headquarters at Cambridge; of more than 300 staff at least 70 overwinter in the five British bases in the Antarctic. However, British scientific efforts there are dwarfed by those of the United States and Russia. The German and Japanese facilities and equipment are luxurious by comparison with those of BAS ships and bases. But BAS today has a considerable reputation for polar expertise and is still one of the leaders in Antarctic research. Until recently, the Survey was in decline as funds became more limited, but now the revival of its strength and the reprieve of Endurance are directly linked to the policies of Margaret Thatcher's Conservative government in the Falklands. So, Britain's longer-term prospects in Antarctica as a whole are tied to the narrower perspective of the British stance over the Falklands, known today as the Fortress Falklands policy.

This comes at a time when international interest in Antarctica is increasing. More countries are seeking to join the Antarctic Treaty, which came into existence in 1961. The Treaty bans the use of the continent and waters around it for military purposes and the testing of weapons there and declares that the fruits of scientific work should be shared internationally. So far it has been a success. The superpowers, Russia and America, co-operate fully, and so do the seven countries who have made claims to territory in Antarctica itself; among them are three with rival claims to the Antarctic Peninsula: Britain, Chile and Argentina.

The Falklands conflict underlined the fragility of the state of international harmony in Antarctica in that two founder-members of the Treaty, Britain and Argentina, had gone to war on the fringes of the Antarctic Ocean over a territorial dispute that extends to parts of Antarctica itself. So here I am one of the 13 Royal Marines on board to protect Endurance and help facilitate the BAS scientists in their work. The thought of what's ahead excites me, especially in the knowledge that I will be treading ground made famous by so many important people and events that have shaped our future and knowledge. To become part of that is such an amazing, exciting adventure.

Before we knew it, we were approaching Stanley Harbour in the Falklands. I will always remember my thoughts as I set eyes on this unassuming place in the middle of nowhere, hardly known to anyone until brought to light from the battle for the island. A British colony of such strategic importance.

Finally, once again we were on dry land, and we were egar to get ashore and stretch our legs. We had many a good time in the Falklands. I recall one time having been invited to an RAF dance after we had docked. The drinks were only 20p a shot so you can imagine having been at sea for four weeks coming back to such an offer. At the end of the evening, Tony, Mike and I were invited to a Wraf's (Women's Royal Air Force) house, it was a car ride away in the middle of nowhere. After partying into the early hours, it was time to get back to the ship. We were all full of alcohol and we had a bit of a yomp home. Rather than stick to the roads we opted to take a shortcut across some wasteland towards the harbour. After climbing several fences and walking through ground not too dissimilar to that on Dartmoor, we arrived at the harbour.

I don't know what got into me but for some reason I decided to throw one of the three emergency life rings into the water to show the others how the light on the ring reacted to the saltwater and completed the battery circuits, enabling the light to work. To my surprise this didn't happen, so I proceeded to throw the other life buoys in the water, mumbling about how poor maintenance was on the emergency life buoys. We then decided to take up trampolining on the fenders the ship was moored up against. It wasn't long before naval security came running up the docks to try and arrest us for jumping on the fenders and throwing the emergency buoys in the water. Knowing that in the Navy the harbour master was god, we scarpered onto the ship straight to bed before they could identify us. Unfortunately, the complaint had been made and Tony and I were hauled up to face the skipper and explain our actions the following morning. Captain Guyer came down to the Marines' mess to get us and gave us a heads up as to why we were being summoned. We were marched into the skipper's office and given a brief lecture on harbour masters' rules on the docks and how it was a serious chargeable offence to disobey those rules and of misappropriating the equipment around the harbour. Then we were asked to explain why we were trampolining on the fenders and why we had thrown all the life buoys in the water. This called for some quick thinking, or we would be in big trouble. Well, sir, I said, as we were approaching the ship I thought I saw someone in trouble in the water, I jumped onto the fender to help and asked Tony to throw in a buoy. It turned out as I got closer to the splashing that it was a couple of seals and not someone as we first suspected. I knew the harbour was renowned to have a good population of seals, so I knew it was a more than feasible excuse. I could see the frustration on the skipper's face, I could tell he wanted to make an example of us for misbehaving but couldn't prove this wasn't the case. And what about the other two emergency buoys found in the water? I've no idea, sir, we only used the one. I knew no one had seen us throw the others in or they would have chased us well before we got to our ship. Well, I don't believe a word of it, but unfortunately, I can't prove otherwise so you boys had better not get into any more mischief or I will come down hard on you, he said. Yes, sir, and we marched out of the office unscathed. As we walked back to the mess deck Captain Guyer said, total bullshit, but good that you didn't end up being deported back to the UK and bring the Corps into disrepute. Don't let it happen again!! No, sir, it won't. It was later found that the route we took to get back to the ship that night was over an uncleared minefield. There were still a lot of fenced off areas in the Falklands waiting to be cleared of mines. What a wild run ashore that night turned out to be.

We remained moored up in Stanley harbour for three days. During this time, we Marines were given a bit of freedom to brush up on our map reading skills and get out on yomps around Stanley. Mac, one of my good friends who later became RSM of 42 Commando, was keen to learn to dive and, on the way over to the Falklands he went diving with some of the Navy boys but had a bad experience so I assured him I would build his confidence again and I promised to give him some one-on-one time as often as I could.

Lying at the east end of Stanley Harbour is Stanley's most imposing and iconic shipwreck. Known as Lady Liz, the ship was launched in Sunderland in the UK in 1879 and suffered damage whilst rounding Cape Horn in 1913. She limped into Stanley for repairs, but the high cost prevented any being carried out. After various moorings in Stanley Harbour, a violent gale in 1936 forced the Lady Liz into her current resting place. She is grounded resting with a slight list to one side. When the tide is in you can get to a depth of around six to 10 metres around her. This was the perfect place to take Mac on his dive experience and build up his confidence in the water again. We got into one of the inflatable Gemini boats with some scuba diving gear and headed out to the Lady Liz. The dolphins were coming with us as we sped towards her. The dolphins were enjoying chasing and crossing the bow of the boat as if teasing us to go faster. They always seem to stay just within a few feet of the bow, jumping in front. Once we got to the shipwreck, I anchored on the shallow side of the boat almost on the coral beach. We could stand waist deep and we kitted up and got into the water. I went through a few safety checks with Mac and then eased him under the water face to face to ensure him all was good. I brought with me a stick about half the length of a broomstick and gave it to Mac so he could poke around with it to take his mind off the fear of being totally submerged under water. I would point out various underwater life like crabs and shrimp so he could poke around engrossed in the colourful corals and various fish etc. all the time moving him deeper around the wreck. After some time I stopped him and with us both kneeling on the bottom I got him to look up at the wreck and he realised he was no longer at a depth he could stand up in but in fact he was some 10 metres deep. We remained in the water exploring for another 30 minutes or more before making our way back to our small Gemini boat. Once we finished the dive, he was over the moon that he had conquered his fear of going deep and from there on was always asking to dive whenever I was going in myself. It reminded me of the enjoyment I got from teaching people to dive. The happy look on their faces when they achieve their dreams. It's a great feeling.

* * *

CHAPTER 9

On the eastward journey to South Georgia, Endurance crossed the path taken by Captain James Cook on his second voyage to the Southern Ocean, very possibly the greatest voyage of navigation and discovery undertaken by a single commander, and here we were taking the same path. By today's standards his achievements were remarkable; by the standards of their own time, just over two centuries ago, they were astonishing. Born in Yorkshire in 1728, the son of a farm labourer, Cook owed his education to John Walker, a Quaker ship owner who became his lifelong patron. Walker sent the young Cook to sea on his colliers out of Whitby, but in the winter paid for him to study mathematics and navigation.

Although he was offered a command by Walker in 1755, Cook joined the Royal Navy as an able seaman and quickly rose to master. It was he who navigated Admiral Saunders' fleet up the St Lawrence river for the capture of Quebec. Cook's real achievements, however, were in times of peace. These began with his three great voyages of discovery from 1768 to his death in 1779. The first voyage aboard the Endeavour was to the South Pacific to witness the transit of Venus, after which Cook sailed in a figure of eight around New Zealand and charted the coasts, going on to make a detailed survey of the east coast of Australia, and arriving back in England in 1771. Cook's skills at chart-making have never been surpassed. On 13

July 1772 he set sail again with two ships, the Resolution and the Adventure, to search for the great southern continent (his curiosity about this land, part of marine mythology since classical times, had been roused on the previous voyage). No such continent was found, but the journey saw a great advance in the health of ships' companies on long hauls. On the first southern journey Cook's men had suffered dreadfully from scurvy and on the journey home from Batavia in the East Indies were decimated by malaria and dysentery. Cook ensured that they had plenty of fruit, which was gathered in revictualling stops in New Zealand and the Pacific Islands. The benefits of eating fresh citrus fruits to combat scurvy had long been known, but he was the first to apply this knowledge systematically. Cook's ships crossed the Antarctic Circle (66°30'S) and on 30 January 1774 Resolution reached 71°10'S at longitude 106°54/W. In his journal Cook wrote: I will not say it was impossible to get farther to the south; but the attempting it would have been a dangerous and rash enterprise, and what, I believe no man in my situation would have thought of.

Indeed, no one got further south than this until James Weddell half a century later. Off what is now known as Thurston Island, Cook was confronted by a wall of heavy pack ice, and he speculated that it would continue uninterrupted to the South Pole. Again, no one reached as far south in that part of the Antarctic Ocean as he did until two American ice-breakers, the Staten Island and the Glacier, reached the same point in 1961. During this voyage he revolutionized the use of the chronometer for reckoning positions of latitude. In the final phase of this journey, Resolution rounded the Horn from the Pacific and, avoiding the Falklands, headed towards South Georgia, which was claimed for George III. Cook then sailed east and south, discovering the Candlemas and South Sandwich Islands, and headed home. He was elected a member of the Royal Society and awarded the Copley medal for his work on the prevention of scurvy. Cook made one more journey: with the Resolution and Adventure he set out to search for the North-West Passage from the Pacific end. It was on this journey early in 1779 that he was killed in a scuffle at Kealakekua Bay in Hawaii after one of Discovery's boats was stolen by the islanders.

No member of the Royal Navy enjoys such a high reputation internationally as Cook, despite the emphasis in British history texts on martial heroes like Nelson and Drake. He was simply the first, and possibly the greatest, Antarctic navigator and scientist. He was the founder of a tradition of precise observation and measurement in the southern oceans, a tradition inherited by Scott, Shackleton and the BAS. It is a tradition that now might be jeopardised by bureaucratic cheese-paring and the narrow perceptions and policies over the South Atlantic following the Falklands conflict.

Heading towards South Georgia, life aboard Endurance settled quickly into the seagoing routine. The helicopter crew maintained their machines and we trained with small arms shooting out into the wilderness. You could quite easily sit back and become bored with life onboard, but I liked to dwell on the history of where we are going and how it must have been for others before us.

On reaching South Georgia, the first task was to resupply the scientists who were at the base on Bird Island, the smallest of the permanent British bases and the main BAS centre in South Georgia. It is devoted almost exclusively to the life sciences, principally the observation and study of seals, penguins and albatrosses. The wind was beginning to build to a small gale when Endurance reached the island. In the early morning, the clouds were ragged curtains of vapour over the jagged bluish mountains along the coast. Beneath the peaks some still covered with snow, was the occasional lash of bright green vegetation. At first, we were not sure whether the helicopters would be launched — no flying is permitted when the wind reaches speeds of more than forty knots — but eventually it was decided to go ahead despite conditions. Myself and four other marines were the first grounded, followed by the scientists and some of the matelots.

The most impressive thing about the base was the efficiency and economy with which every space was used. The next thing was the range of decoration: pin-ups, and pictures of the finest bird and mammal specimens the scientists had photographed themselves around the base. A long shot from the pink bulkhead and Page 3 girls in our mess deck! Apart from the pinboards, which marked each man's territory, there were rows and rows of bookcases containing almost every conceivable form of literature. A great deal of care had been taken to insulate the living and sleeping quarters, although Bird Island does not suffer such cold temperatures as bases further south. Entering the porch there is a double door, like an air chamber, and then a corridor to the main room. Up to 10 people work at the base in summer and five or six in winter. Much of the work in the long, dark winter months is devoted to maintaining and repairing the huts and facilities, but otherwise the station's primary commitment is to the Biological Investigations of Marine Antarctic Systems and Stocks (BIOMASS) programme run by the Scientific Committee on Antarctic Research (SCAR), which now has 15 member nations.

BIOMASS concentrates mainly on the potential harvest from krill. According to the scientists they told us that the birds and seals of South Georgia eat one and a half million tons of seafood a year. I thought to myself, they would eat a lot less if they relied on Endurance to feed them. One thing I will say though is Endurance could do with some of Captain Cook's nutritional expertise. Mealtimes occasionally produced some of the most tired-looking vegetables I have seen in my life. Chips, cabbage and sprouts were mounds of dark-brown mush, and the soups, which the steward's fantasy graced with a rich variety of names, wore the uniform grey-green of Port Stanley harbour on a wet Sunday. Eggs, the constant factor in each nautical breakfast, always had a distinctly sulphurous smell. Not that I am casting any doubts on the culinary ingenuity of the ship's cooks and stewards: but I know I have done better when out in the field eating dehydrated food with the American Seals; I mean, I thought they were bad but hey, give me a dehydrated chicken supreme dinner with homemade spices and cooked by one's own skills any day of the week. Endurance has the longest regular deployment out of home waters of any ship in the Navy, and resupply with fresh food is a constant problem for any ship operating in the South Atlantic. She has to carry ten months' stores of food and equipment. However, for many stomachs the end of the ship's deployment is more than adequately summed up by her name. But hey, no point fantasizing about a medium rare steak, we were here to resupply the base and deliver the new scientists.

South Georgia is the most attractive of the Antarctic islands in the variety of its landscape and animal and bird life. In late summer the distant mountains and hills radiate a brilliant green, though the peaks are perpetually covered in snow. Many of the highest mountains have still to be climbed, for expeditions to the interior can be ambushed by sudden changes in weather from bright sunshine to ferocious snowstorms. Legend has it that the island was discovered in 1512 by the Florentine explorer Amerigo Vespucci, who also claimed to have discovered the American continent. An English merchant, Antonio de la Roché, is believed to have sighted it in April 1675, and a bullion ship sailing from Lima to Cadiz, which was blown off course, is supposed to have seen it in June-July 1756. But the first person to survey the northern coast and land was James Cook in January 1775. He appears to have landed in Possession Bay and then sailed to the large inlet with arms stretching east and west, which he named Cumberland Bay. His naturalists and geographer gave detailed accounts of the landscape and animal life. Tucked below the entrance to Cumberland East Bay are Grytviken, for sixty years the capital of the Norwegian whaling industry in the Antarctic, and King Edward Point, where the magistrate responsible for the Falkland Islands Dependencies has his seat. Anyone wishing to land on South Georgia must seek clearance for immigration from the magistrate, an authority vested in the British troop commander on the island after the Falklands conflict. Before this the base commander of the BAS team at Grytviken assumed the magistrate's mantle. It was the failure of a party of Argentine scrap-metal dealers to seek his permission to land at Leith in March 1982 that heralded the opening of hostilities between Britain and Argentina. The contract to dispose of scrap at the whaling station there had been won quite legitimately by the firm of Señor Constantino Davidoff of Buenos Aires. He applied to the British embassy and consular authority in Argentina for his men to travel to South Georgia to begin work in early 1982. Once they arrived off the island, they ignored the magistrate at King Edward Point and on 19 March went direct to Leith in Stromness Bay. One of the party raised the Argentine flag there. Towards the end of March the scrap-metal dealers, among whom there were almost certainly military personnel, were reinforced by the tender Bahia Paraiso. On the last day of the month Endurance landed a party of Royal Marines at Grytviken under the command of Lieutenant Keith Mills. The day after the Falklands fell to the Argentines, the Bahia Paraiso appeared off King Edward Point, accompanied by a corvette. The magistrate was asked to surrender. As the corvette rounded the point, she was hit by a fusillade of 84-mm Carl Gustav rockets. It was the last thing the Argentines expected. Not only had Keith Mills' ambush taken them completely by surprise, but it appeared at the time that they did not know the marines were there at all.

A three-hour battle ensued in which two Argentine helicopters were shot down and several Argentine soldiers killed before the British were defeated. The scientists and civilians had hidden in the church in Grytviken. According to the BAS chronicler, Bob Headland, they were given 20 minutes to pack and were then taken aboard the Bahia Paraiso. The last to leave were the magistrate, Keith Mills and Headland himself. Just over three weeks later, on 26 April, British forces retook South Georgia. The operation had a chaotic start when two helicopters trying to land a reconnaissance party of SAS on the Fortuna Glacier, west of Stromness Bay, crashed. Their crews and the SAS men had to be rescued. A patrol setting out in rubber boats fared little better and had to be recovered. Eventually British marines and SAS men were landed, and the helicopters from Endurance attacked and damaged the aged Argentine submarine Santa Fé, which they found on the surface in open water at the mouth of Cumberland Bay. Hours later, 200 Argentine servicemen and civilians surrendered to the captain of HMS Antrim and Nick Barker, the then captain of Endurance. The Argentine commander, Alfredo Astiz, was wanted by the European Court of Human Rights for his involvement with one of the most notorious torture centres, the marine engineering academy on the outskirts of Buenos Aires, in the so called 'dirty war' waged by the Argentine military against dissidents and guerrillas from 1976 to 1982.

One of his men was less fortunate: he was shot by his British escort who believed he was about to open the sea cocks of the Santa Fé and scuttle her. Later, Astiz disappeared in Brazil as he and his fellow prisoners were being taken back to Argentina. It is worth recalling these events because a disproportionate amount of wreckage from the conflict is still strewn along the shore at Grytviken and Leith. This old abandoned whaling station has an eerie feel about it when you walk around the empty skeletons of buildings. The occasional roar of the huge elephant seals, of which there seems to be hundreds of them just flopped on the shore or half in the water. As well as being home to most of the world's Antarctic fur seals, South Georgia is also home to 50% of the global population of southern elephant seals (around 400,000). They are the largest of all seal species. Males typically weigh six times more than females and can weigh up to 4.5 tonnes. They are surprisingly mobile too, particularly when challenging each other. Between 1904 and 1965 some 175,250 whales were processed at South Georgia shore stations. In the whole of the Antarctica region some 1,432,862 animals were taken between 1904 and 1978, when hunting of the larger species ceased.

The site operated for almost 60 years and over 53,000 whale carcasses were landed and processed here at Grytviken alone. Although founded by a Norwegian, the name "Grytviken" is actually Swedish! It means "Pot Bay" and was named by the Swedish survey expedition of 1902 because they found several old British try pots here – large vessels used to render down seal blubber. The whaling station was abandoned in 1966 as uneconomical after stocks of whales in the region had dropped to critical levels due to over-hunting, and there are no permanent residents. However, a few officials do live here during the tourist season to manage the South Georgia Museum and the post office, which is located here; it is a fascinating place to visit. There is more famous Antarctic human history to discover at Grytviken. Just outside the settlement lies the grave of Sir Ernest Shackleton, the famous Antarctic explorer, who died here from a sudden heart attack in 1922. There is also a marker next to his grave, marking the spot where the ashes of his key crew member and fellow explorer Frank Wild were interred.

Well before I finish rabbiting on about South Georgia Island, its history and its beauty, I have to tell you about the penguins. Never could I have ever imagined being amongst so many penguins. Particularly the king penguin. Standing just under a metre tall with their smart grey suits, black heads punctuated with large gold commas and salmon bills, kings are one of the handsomest penguin species. South Georgia is home to around 450,000 pairs of them, or somewhere between a third and half the world›s population. To be stood in the middle surrounded by these guys was an experience to behold. The feeling of being so at one with nature›s beauty was overwhelming. I will never forget sitting on a rock, opening my flask of hot soup and watching two king penguins tease and toil a large elephant seal. They would each approach it from opposite sides, the seal not knowing which side he was being pecked at, the kings being so much faster, just antagonizing him as he twisted from side to side trying to fend off the kings. Another memorable connection with the penguins was with the little macaroni penguins. Adults weigh on average 5.5kg (12lb) and are 70cm (28in) in length. They would come running up to us and peck us on the legs. We would pick them up and throw them back in the water like throwing a rugby ball, but they would return each time for another throw. Unbelievable little creatures! I'm convinced they were having so much fun.

Penguins are amongst the oldest inhabitants of Antarctica. A fossil of a penguin has been found in the Antarctic Peninsula that dates back sixty million years. It is believed that the beasts were man-sized then, about five and a half feet tall. According to some experts, the bone structure indicates that their predecessors were capable of flight, but today they are more like aquatic birds as their wings are incapable of flexing like those of birds of flight and are used instead as paddles or flippers. In St Andrew's Bay and the neighbouring Royal Bay, the king penguins gave wonderfully gymnastic displays diving through the surf and gliding out to sea.

We remained on South Georgia Island for two days whilst the scientists did their thing. It was during this time when I was invited on a dive with the scientists. However, our dive equipment was somewhat different. They had normal scuba equipment with the separate demand valve and mask, whereas the navy equipment was a full face mask with a built in demand valve. Also, the air cylinders for normal scuba equipment consists of one cylinder with an octopus as a spare demand valve and the top of the cylinder positioned at the back of the head. The Navy, however, consists of two cylinders upside down – one is used for breathing, the second is used as a spare so when you feel you are running out of air, you reach your arm around the back, open the spare cylinder till it equalises and both cylinders are now half full of air and you close the spare cylinder off again. This can be done three times before it's time to return to the surface. Under normal conditions this works very well; however, this was some of the first dives in ice conditions with navy equipment for longer periods underwater.

I suddenly came to the stage where it was difficult to breathe. I found myself slightly isolated from the other divers as I reached my arm around to equalise the pressure. Usually when you find the last few breaths difficult it's time to equalise and get more pressure into the cylinder; however, when trying to do this I found the cylinder screw top was frozen solid and I could not open it. I had a full face mask which meant I couldn't share air with the other divers so in the end I had to resort to shooting to the surface and ripping my face mask off in order to breathe. This was quite a scary moment. Obviously when diving you should not shoot to the surface and must consider decompression stops on the way up to avoid the bends, which is when the nitrogen bubbles in your blood swell up as you surface. This could be lethal. More so when you are out in the middle of the Antarctic with no real facility to treat you, no decompression chambers out there. All of these firsts were recorded in my reports, and I believe now when the navy dive in such extreme conditions they use scuba equipment so as to avoid these types of occurrences.

We left South Georgia and headed across the Scotia Sea towards the Sandwich Islands. I was looking forward to visiting all these islands. Our journey was to take us from South Georgia to the South Sandwich Islands then onto South Orkney Islands then on to South Shetland Islands and King George Island and the Deception Island. Particularly the volcanically heated water at Deception Island. The last confirmed eruption took place in 1970, and further eruptions are expected though are notoriously unpredictable. The two eruptions in the 1960s took everyone by surprise, not least the scientists at the British and Chilean stations at the time who had their huts partially destroyed and were rather keen on being rescued! Getting ashore on this volcano was another unusual experience. There we were in the middle of the Antarctic, surrounded by ice and snow for as far as the eye could see, yet on the parts we stood there was numerous ponds of warm steamy water you could bathe in naked and feel warm. This whole area of the Antarctic is just stunning scenery. The sheer volume of the massive ice glaciers and icebergs are just a sight to behold. The thundering noise as the massive glaciers break and crash into the water are as eerie as they are spectacular. Our journey took us to a place called Rothera base station on Adelaide Island. Adelaide Island is built on a rock promontory at the southern tip of the Wormald Ice Piedmont, Rothera Research Station is situated on Adelaide Island to the west of the Antarctic Peninsula. Adelaide Island is 1,860km south of the Falkland Islands and 1,630km south-east of Punta Arenas, Chile. The island, which is 140km long, is mountainous and heavily glaciated. Its highest peak is 2,565 metres. This was particularly good for us as Marines because we were allowed off the ship and given some free time to escape the confines of our small cramped mess deck whilst our onboard scientists resupplied their colleagues.

The station operates throughout the year. In summer, the population peaks at just over 100 people, while during the winter months, from April to mid-October, a 22-strong team continues the science work and maintains Rothera's infrastructure.

Staff on station include marine and terrestrial biologists, meteorologists, electronics engineers, a dive officer and a boating officer, a chef, a doctor, vehicle and generator mechanics, electricians, plumbers, builders, field assistants, communications managers and a station management team.

Summer temperatures are typically between zero and +5°C, and in winter range from –5°C to – 20°C, but because of its coastal location and the Southern Ocean low-pressure weather systems, temperatures can vary widely at any time of year.

You can find sea ice at Rothera from late May to late November, although it takes prolonged periods of calm conditions for ice to form and become fast. Prevailing winds are northerlies, reaching gale force on around 70 days a year. While it can snow at any time of year, in recent years the main snowfall has come at the end of winter. Rain occasionally falls at Rothera.

Because the station is just south of the Antarctic Circle, it is light for 24 hours a day during summer, and for a few weeks in winter the sun never rises above the horizon.

The station's coastal location means that staff see a good range of Antarctic birds and mammals. Adélies are the most numerous penguin species around Rothera, with chinstrap and gentoos occasionally present in the summer. The emperor penguin is seen infrequently, with sightings most likely between September and November.

There are breeding populations of Dominican gull (three pairs) and South Polar skua (15 pairs or more). Antarctic terns and Wilson's petrels are present offshore through the summer months but nest on higher mountain ridges. The blue-eyed shag, which breeds on several offshore islands, can be seen whenever the sea is not frozen.

Weddell seals, which are present year-round, are the most obvious mammal around the station. Pups are born on the sea ice in late September. Crabeater and elephant seals are also present, fur seals arrive in varying numbers at the end of summer, and although leopard seals are present all year round, they are seen only infrequently.

Small numbers of minke and humpback whales are seen in Ryder Bay each summer, and in some years minke are spotted almost every day. A family of orcas, which lives in the Marguerite Bay area, is usually seen from the station several times during the summer.

The station is reached by air or sea. Today, most people fly to Rothera on the BAS Dash 7 aircraft, either from Stanley in the Falkland Islands (about five hours) or Punta Arenas, Chile (about four and a half hours). BAS ships bring passengers and cargo to Rothera at least twice each summer, and sailing time from Stanley is around four days.

Ship visits are vital because they bring essential supplies, from food, fuel and scientific equipment to vehicles, building supplies and personal possessions.

A new upgraded wharf replaces a smaller structure built in the 1980s as part of the Antarctic Infrastructure Modernisation Programme, commissioned by the Natural Environment Council (NERC), part of UK Research and Innovation (UKRI). The 74-metre wharf is designed to accommodate the new polar research vessel, RRS Sir David Attenborough. With its enhanced cargo handling facilities, including a larger crane, the new wharf has enabled more efficient loading and unloading of supplies, as well as the deployment of small boats used for scientific diving and marine research operations.

Staff eat meals together in the central dining room; lunch and dinner are made by the chefs. On Saturdays, there is a more formal dinner: dress is smart casual and everyone enjoys a multi-course meal. And although the chefs do not have access to fresh ingredients, they prepare nutritious, high quality food every day.

Station life is busy, and often dictated by the weather. As a result, a traditional UK-style working week is impractical at Rothera.

We got away for three days and two nights out into the frozen wilderness. It was during this time that we came across a huge, buried crevasse. Because we were traversing across an unknown ground and frozen landscape, we would ski in a single file linked together with a rope. I was the lead skier at the time, and as I carefully made my way ahead, one of my ski poles suddenly broke through the snow and into nothing. I froze and raised my hand, halting the rest of the guys behind me and proceeded to remove my backpack and lie on my belly so as to spread my weight. I used my ski pole to enlarge the hole to try and assess my predicament. It's not unheard of in these conditions to find one suddenly disappear through the snow into a massive hole covered by a crust of snow. This is why we move in this unknown environment tied together. So, we had found a huge crevasse. It wasn't long before we had secured some ropes and we belayed down into the huge area of ice. Once inside it was an amazing sight. It was just a massive room of pure ice, and the blue of the ice was accentuated as the light hit. It seemed to go on as far as the eye could see. We spent a little time taking photos and admiring the scale of where we were before moving on.

Once we were miles away from the base camp and totally out of sight we dug in snow holes and spent the next three days living in the snow holes and exploring during the day and night. A great time was had and a far cry from being stuck on board the ship. Plus, finally we could do our own cooking and away from that horrible stuff they were feeding us on board.

The black nights with crystal clear skies and the sparkling stars, the complete silence was heavenly. Time passed extremely quickly and it was soon time to head back to base camp. Our trek back took a good eight hours of skiing and we could hear the dogs as we neared the base camp. I'm a real dog lover and currently have three lovely west highland terriers that I couldn't live without.

Annex II to the Environmental Protocol (Conservation of Antarctic Fauna and Flora) required that dogs were removed from Antarctica by April 1994. This ban was introduced because of concern that dogs might introduce diseases such as canine distemper that might be transferred to seals, and that they could break free and disturb or attack the wildlife. It was also thought to be inconsistent for the Protocol to have strict controls on the introduction of non-native species, but at the same time allow huskies to be bred and used in Antarctica.

Dogs were taken to the Antarctic on the early 'heroic age' expeditions at the turn of the 20th Century. They were instrumental in helping the Norwegian explorer Amundsen and his team to be the first to reach the South Pole in 1911. The fact that the Norwegians were good and experienced dog handlers was thought by many experts to be one of the main reasons that they were able to reach the pole before Scott and his team. Since those days, dogs have been used extensively for polar travel and for the support of scientific work. Although dogs were slower than vehicles, they were considered to be safer as they were not so heavy and it was thought that huskies also had an awareness of crevasses. Sledge dogs were used by BAS in the Antarctic from 1945. The original dogs were imported from the Arctic, from Labrador in Canada, and there were small additions in stock from Greenland (1954 and 1961). Careful records were kept of the breeding to avoid producing dogs affected by hereditary disorders. Dogs were also exchanged between bases in Antarctica (eg Argentinian base, San Martin) in order to maintain genetic diversity. At British stations, dogs were generally fed on seal meat and therefore a certain number of seals were killed each year to support them. The dogs were gradually replaced by mechanised transport during the 60s and 70s and skidoos became the main vehicle for transporting field parties overland.

In the 1980s and early 1990s, a small number of dogs were kept at Rothera Research Station for recreational purposes. The dogs were well looked after and gave station personnel the chance to get a feel for what the earlier explorers and scientists would have experienced. The dogs were also considered to be good for morale, which is important in an environment where people are away from home for periods of over two years. There was considerable resistance from station personnel when the legislation for the removal of the dogs was put in place.

The 14 remaining dogs were finally removed from Rothera in February 1994. To mark the end of the era, the dogs spent the last season doing what they did best, pulling a sledge as a working team in support of a surveying project on Alexander Island. When the dogs finally departed Rothera, special husky kennels were built and fitted inside the BAS Dash 7 aircraft for the five-hour flight to the Falkland Islands. The dogs spent several weeks adapting to the warmer climate and new surroundings, experiencing grass, sheep and children for the first time. They flew from the Falklands to the UK on a special RAF Tristar flight. Once again the dogs received a warm welcome to the UK, this time becoming media stars in all the national papers. Once quarantine was completed the final leg of their journey took them to Quebec in Canada, courtesy of British Airways.

Of the 13 dogs who arrived in Canada, five died within the first year due to infection and disease. Unfortunately, it was not possible to breed from any of the remaining dogs and the last two died in 2001. Sadly, the end of an era for the British Antarctic husky dogs. I knew the dogs first hand and can only admire the resilience of these animals. They were kept outside and curled up covered in snow in sub-zero temperatures, yet in the mornings when you walked to feed them they were so happy to see you. Yes, ok we were bringing them food but still they seemed almost like household pets. I could fully understand how they boosted morale.

Our time was finished here in Rothera base camp and we were soon off again surveying uncharted waters, which brings me onto another funny incident that happened during my time in the Antarctic. Probably a mistake on the navy side to leave marines in charge of the bridge; however, there was one time that our captain was in charge of the bridge together with Tony and myself. At the time we were doing a hydrographic survey of uncharted waters. This involved dragging a sonar at the rear of the ship mapping the bottom of the ocean and sending depth signals back to the bridge monitoring system. We had a young navy boy who was on duty watching the change in depth. Unfortunately, the poor lad was not at his station but instead listening to us three talking about experiences and what our plans were when we got back to a commando unit. By chance he popped into the survey room just to check the depth equipment and suddenly shouted out the depth of the water rapidly getting shallow at an alarming rate. Captain Guyer threw the ship into reverse and although I'm sure it helped a little, it didn't stop the ship from hitting an underwater mountain. There was a loud scraping noise as the ship listed slightly to one side; panic took over and all hands on deck. We eventually came to a stop and the divers were summoned to quickly check the hull of the ship, I was one of the divers. Being in charge of the diving on board, I went in the water to check the hull. Fortunately, there was no damage; however, the sonar had got wrapped around the prop at the rear. We spent some time underwater trying to untangle the sonar from the prop. This was not a pleasant job because we were in waters surrounded by icebergs having to try and untangle a very tangled sonar wire, when your fingers and head felt painfully cold. We had others on watch with thunder flashes – these are like small sticks of dynamite ready to throw in the water on sight of any predators like large seals etc. It is not unheard-of divers being attacked by seals – they can be very aggressive creatures when intruders are in their territory. Needless to say, I was a happy man when we eventually finished untangling the sonar and I was once again out of my drysuit and back into warm clothing. That said, I will never forget the pain in my hands and behind my nails on rewarming. I thought my resistance to interrogation training was bad. This actually brought tears to my eyes.

We had some fun times during our deployment on HMS Endurance too, especially at the various different countries we stopped off at to have a little light R and R (Rest and Recuperation). Two places that stand out are Rio de Janerio and Madeira. Rio because there is so much to see like Copacabana beach, Ipanema beach, Christ the redeemer, Sugarloaf mountain to name just a few, and the atmosphere in Rio is fantastic.

When we docked at Rio we had our first night out for a good while and we ended up finding a bar which at first sight looked quite good but once inside it was like a scene from the George Clooney movie From Dusk till Dawn – full of bikers and girls, who turned into vampires after midnight – but wow, what a night we had. The funniest bit of all was at the end of the night Mac and I escaped away from the girls and headed back towards the ship. We were so tired and drunk. It wasn't long before we were fast asleep. Unbeknown to us, one of the girls from the bar had followed us back and unbelievably got through security and on board the ship, but she mistakenly woke the navigator in the officers' quarters, jumping in his bed saying Mucho Grande, which was the nickname they gave to Mac in the bar. As you can imagine, this didn't go down so well and there was questions in the morning during first parade. The funny part was the way it was described at first parade, explaining that the navigator had some half-dressed woman in his bed screaming Mucho Grande. He was not impressed but the rest of the ship's detachment were in stitches. Although it did raise a lot of questions over security on board the ship, it's understandable how she got past the local guards but how she got on board our ship was not good for the duty watch.

Madeira was another eventful stopover. When we arrived and docked the word had gotten out that HMS Endurance had a detachment of Royal Marines on board, so the local US Marines invited us over to their villa for a party. They were holding a black-tie event but unfortunately, none of us had black tie attire. Obviously not expecting to go anywhere posh during our detachment on HMS Endurance; consequently we all turned up in jeans and T-shirts. We arrived mid-afternoon and were shown around the villa by the US Marines. It was quite an impressive villa with bulletproof electric drop-down shutters on all of the doors and windows. It was obvious that things were not done half-heartedly and a US marine base abroad had to have high security. It wasn't long before we were into the alcohol. Most of the boys had been given a bottle of beer whilst Mac and I sat at the bar talking to the US Marine barman. He asked us if we drank tequila and of course any challenge laid down, particularly by the US Marines, had to be taken with open arms, so we said yes of course, to which he reached down and pulled a special bottle out, explaining that this had the worm in and that once opened had to be drunk. No problem, we said, as he scrunched up the bottle top and began to pour us a shot each. For the next hour we sat chatting, constantly taking the salt, tequila and a bite of lemon just to help it go down until finally the bottle was empty. We won't lie, we were feeling it a little, especially a bottle of tequila between three of us in under an hour, but hey. The barman reached down and pulled out another bottle. Hey I said, I thought that was your only special bottle. Nope, are you saying you've had enough. What and let you girls beat us? we said laughing. Bring it on. During this time all the other guests started to arrive, and we had some high flyers with their wives dressed in long cocktail dresses starting to appear. The barman seemed to suddenly make himself scarce. I think we had finished him with the tequila, so Mac and I finished the remains of the bottle and joined the party. I was chatting with the lads and mingling in the party when I heard a loud scream from a lady and a huge splash as Mac picked up this female and leaped into the pool, both fully clothed. Then came the loud shout from the American General. That man has got my goddamn wife in the pool.

That was the start of an eventful party and a great introduction to the US Marines. For the next two days we had plenty of competitions with the US Marines, granted they were very good at lifting heavyweights, but when it came to heart and lung training, we would leave them standing; but at the end of the day it was a good bonding session with them. When we were due to leave, the general came to visit the ship. He was piped on board and taken up to the officer's mess, he later asked to come down to the Marines' quarters to speak with us, and he and his fellow marines had brought myself and Mac a nice gift. On one of our visits, they showed us around the US embassy and in the embassy, I had seen a leather drop-down Scroll and written on it said: The only thing a marine feels when he kills someone is the recoil of his rifle. And Mac had seen a large wooden plaque with the US marines pushing the flag up, upon it says, these colours don't run. During the visit we said we liked them, and they had sneakily pinched them from the Embassy and brought them down as a gift for us when we parted. That was a really nice gesture and a great end to our visit.

Figure 24 HMS Endurance

Figure 25 One of the two wasp helicopters off Endurance landing on an iceberg

Figure 26 This is what we were ploughing through despite not being an ice breaker

Figure 27 Seriously we were not an ice breaker but still going

Figure 28 Preparing to welcome the skipper's guests on board. He liked showing off his Marines

Figure 29 Volcano Deception Islands

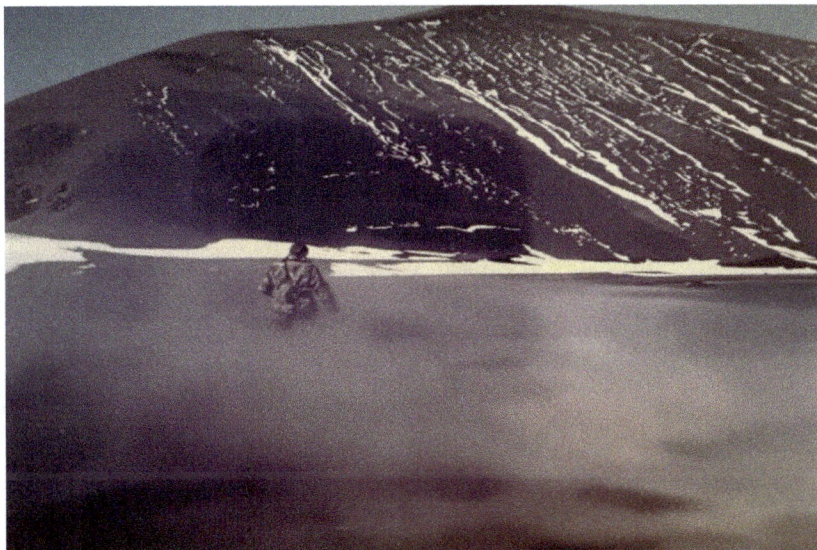

Figure 30 Steam coming from volcano In middle of Antarctic

Figure 31Endurance inside volcano

Figure 32 The Falklands out and about

Figure 33 So many penguins

Figure 34 Looks amazing but the smell oh my

Figure 35 Just playing with you, sir

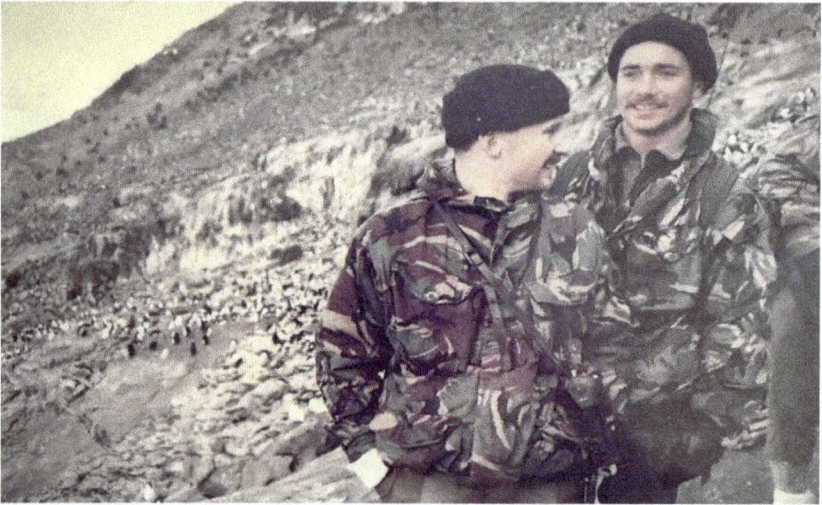

Figure 36 Penguins as far as the eye can see

Figure 37 Christmas Day in our Pink mess deck

Figure 38 At last away from the ship for a few days

Figure 39 The crevasse we found

Figure 40 Inside the crevasse

Figure 41 Climb down into crevasse

* * *

CHAPTER 10

At the end of our detachment with HMS Endurance we were shipped back to our units, back to 42 Commando at Bickleigh Barracks. Having been almost two years with HMS Endurance going back to a commando unit was refreshing. Away from the pink painted accommodation and the constant rocking that comes from living on the water. It was good to see our colleagues again. Back to Plymouth and the famous Union Street. Union Street in Plymouth, Devon, is a long straight street connecting the city centre to Devonport, the site of Plymouth's naval base and docks. Originally the home of wealthy people, it later became an infamous red-light district and the location of most of the city's nightlife. Designed by John Foulston, it was laid out between 1812 and 1820 as a grand boulevard to connect the three towns of Plymouth, East Stonehouse and Devonport. Today Union Street forms part of the A374. For some years after its construction, Union Street was the home of the wealthy. Despite its upper-class associations, Union Street was the location of the first outbreaks in Plymouth of cholera in the 1849 epidemic. At the time, these outbreaks in July of that year were believed to be caused by works connected with the new Millbay railway station, during which the drains of several houses had become blocked, and their lower premises overflowed with sewage.

It was the continuing development along and around Union Street that led to the merger of the Three Towns in 1914, and the granting of Plymouth's city status in 1928.

Frequented by sailors from all over the world, it was once known as one of the West Country's most infamous streets and red-light districts. Much of the area was destroyed by German bombing in World War II, more by widening and slum clearance work.

In 1898 the Palace Theatre opened as a music hall in Union Street. It was damaged by fire only eight months after opening but re-opened in 1899 as the New Palace Theatre of Varieties. In 1961 it was converted to a bingo hall and continued in this use and as a theatre until 1983 when it became "The Academy" disco.

In May 2006 a police operation showed that Class A drugs were being used and dealt there and it closed as a result The building is Grade II listed and in 2008 it was included on a list by the Victorian Society of the UK's ten most endangered and best Victorian and Edwardian buildings. The environment of Union Street – although designated as a local conservation area – is now considerably dilapidated following the closure of the majority of the night leisure businesses in an attempt to control the associated problems of late-night violence and drunkenness. The broken and collapsed historic frontage has fallen into considerable disrepair and many of the businesses associated with servicing the nighttime economy are now vacant. Some limited new developments consist of new housing, low-cost supermarkets and a few remaining late-night venues. Despite the conservation area status, modern developments have not attempted to respect the original historic urban design, with retail parking taking up much of the newer street frontage with higher profile developments more aligned with the aspirations of the Plymouth Plan which are focussed toward the development of links between the city centre and Millbay immediately to the south. It has a noticeable police presence late at night and early into the morning, to control drunk and lively people. As of 2002, it was also patrolled by military police to maintain a degree of integrity among sailors and marines, though it is less frequented by service personnel than it once was. It will always remain in my mind as one of the best run ashores ever. Run ashore is a term used for a night out on the beer. It was one night after our return that Tony and I were having a great night out in Union Street when we bumped into a couple of nice girls who were also part of the Chamber of Commerce group; they were currently organising a world record attempt at the military marathon. Whilst talking to them, they asked us if we were participants; part of our chat up lines were, yes, we're part of the main event. They laughed and said there was no way having come off a deployment on ship that we would be fit enough. So once back at base the following morning we went to see our colour sergeant, a former SBS guy, and he put us straight into the mix. Tony and I were extremely fit during those days and the colour sergeant knew this, hence why he put us as front runners. We only had three days to prepare, whereas all the other units had been training for months. I will always remember that run, we had to do the Plymouth Marathon in boots and carrying 40lb plus rifle which was the 7.62 SLR back then. Recce Troop, who were also doing the run, had been on the TV and radio discussing how they were going to win. Tony and I always thought they were a bit of a primadonna bunch. You had to run as a team of eight and you had to start and finish with the same eight otherwise you were disqualified. Teams would be set off at five-minute intervals. Fortunately for us Recce Troop drew the first straw so they set off first and we were second to set off. Tony and I were the front two, so we set the pace. On this type of run you would usually run for a period of time then a fast march for a period of time and then run again; but because we had Recce Troop in front of us who had the preconception that they were going to win, we decided to run continuously until we had caught up with them. Then when they stopped to march, we would stop to march. This had the desired psychological effect because their troop sergeant dropped back and started to have a go at us saying, can't you set your own pace, boys? This just put us into a more motivated spirit so the next time they stopped to march we continued and overtook them; not only that, but we didn't stop to march anymore. We just ran the whole way and much to Recce Troop's annoyance. We clapped them in 20 minutes after we had arrived. We had broken the world record, showed the girls we could do it and shattered the Recce Troop's dream. What a start back to a commando unit.

Figure 42 Start of the Military Marathon

Figure 43 Winners and Record Breakers

A couple of days after that I had to quickly get my hours of diving in to retain my specialty pay. When you do certain courses like parachutist or diver etc you get additional pay for holding a specific level. In order to keep this pay you had to stay up to date with your skills. I recall my rush to complete my hours underwater to retain my pay. I only had the morning to get two hours underwater to meet my target. I called a good naval colleague of mine who was part of the elite clearance divers' group. We had done many deep dives together using mixed air to enable us to stay deeper longer and lots of fun using the rebreather equipment. A clearance diver was originally a specialist naval diver who used explosives underwater to remove obstructions to make harbours and shipping channels safe to navigate, but the term "clearance diver" was later used to include other naval underwater work. Units of clearance divers were first formed during and after World War II to clear ports and harbours in the Mediterranean and Northern Europe of unexploded ordnance and shipwrecks and booby traps laid by the Germans. Clearance divers have been a permanent force since World War Two, they are the Navy's specialist diving teams and an integral element of the ADF Special Operations structure. He drove over from Devonport Dockyard to 42 Commando barracks to collect me. The problem was at 14:30 I was part of a very important parade and had to be dressed in my blues with peak cap pristine for the parade. So once back at Devonport Dockyard I was quickly dressed into a dry suit and thrown into the murky waters for a two-hour swim whilst he went off and had coffee. I was tied to a surface rope. Later he returned and gave me a few signals just to remind me of what they were. Surface to diver have a number of signalling techniques for communication. For example:

1. pull signal from surface to diver means "Are you ok?", 1 pull return from the diver means "I am ok".
2. pulls from the surface means "stay put", 2 in return means stationary.
3. pulls from the surface means "go down", in return means going down.
4. pulls from the surface means "come up", return means coming up.

Continuous pulls means an emergency come up. From the diver it means an emergency coming up.

There are also a number of signals for directions too so once successfully practised I was pulled out of the water. Time had gone quick, and I was running late. At no cost could I be late, I had to be rigged and ready for the parade. This would have been catastrophic if not. So, my return to 42 Commando was a blue flashing clearance diver Land Rover full throttle not stopping at red lights, dropped off at the gate and me hurtling towards my accommodation to get into blues. It was a very close call, but I succeeded.

Although it was good to get back to a fighting unit it also felt different. I think I had been spoiled with all the adventure and challenges on HMS Endurance. Working as a small team of 13 was very different from being back at a 400-man strong commando unit. It was also the start of another beat up to Norway Arctic training. I spent the next few months getting back into the build-up. Although I did enjoy this it was during my deployment in Norway that I made up my mind to leave the service.

Why? You may ask yourself.

I was constantly being pushed in the direction of promotion. This was something I had very little interest in. I enjoyed doing special assignments and courses. I didn't want to end up in the rat race of promotions. The problem for me and the way I perceived this was there are only so many Marines. In turn there are only so many corporals, sergeants, colour sergeants etc. so each step limits your ability to detach from a unit to cover special operations or assignments because of your responsibilities to your company's responsibilities. I liked where I was and didn't like the thoughts of being directed to where they think I should be.

Also, I vividly recall during another large NATO exercise in Norway under the watchful eyes of umpires in the field. We were the point section leading a path for the rest of the commando unit to follow. We were a team of eight and with light order on skis trail breaking. We were suddenly ambushed. As you would have, given the circumstances, we continued into the attack on skis fighting back, we were stopped by an umpire's whistle. Then we were told to take cover, remove our skis and replace them with snowshoes, then continue the defensive attack on snowshoes. That was the final straw for me. It was so unrealistic and focused on health and safety. Together with the forced direction of where they wanted me to be as opposed to where I wanted to be, it was time. Anyway, I had to make a decision as I was at the point in my career that I needed to decide to sign up for a further nine years and make a career out of this or stand down and return to civilian life. It was an easy decision. The Corps put a lot of effort in to try and keep me signed up, but I had already made a firm decision.

* * *

CHAPTER 11

Because I had completed my apprenticeship and had my trade qualifications as an electrician I was reasonably equipped to get back into the civilian lifestyle. I took some time out with a little diving holiday, what I call sunshine diving, after all the under-ice diving from my Endurance days.

I bought myself a little van and started out as a self-employed electrician. I put adverts in the papers and did leaflet drops to build up work. I was doing quite well for myself when I was approached by a local electrical company. The owner was quite a well-known figure in the local area. He approached me and asked if I would like to come and work with his company. He would provide me with a new van and all my tools etc. This sounded like a good opportunity for me to gain some further experience within a well-established company. So off I went. After around six months I was offered a management position whereby I would take over quoting and designing installations. I was upgraded to a Sierra Cosworth 4x4 which in its day was a nice car. So, I felt I was now beginning to establish myself in civilian life. I was actually starting to like this. During this time, I lived with one of my good friends whom I was in the Marines with, in a place called Statiscombe, Plymstock. The owner of the electrical company was a big rugby fan and decided he wanted to set up a Plymstock rugby club. So, he did. I used to enjoy playing most weekends and because of my general fitness I used to take the teams on physical training sessions doing fireman's carries up and down some of the steepest hills in the area. It was fun. Well at least I thought it was; I'm not sure the others enjoyed it so much.

My youngest brother Malcolm at this time was working in Scotland as a trainee chef. We happened to win a large contract looking after the Royal Western Yacht club. Every year they would hold a big event with hundreds of marquees and boats etc being sold. I managed to get my brother to join me and start his career as an apprentice electrician. Anything was better than the hard slog of trying to become a chef.

I also joined the local British Sub Aqua club in Plymstock. The owner was a member of the "bad lads"; they worked at Fort Bovisand commercial diving centre which at the time was home to the only decompression chamber in the southwest. I used to be invited on many dives with them and enjoyed some great but scary dives. It was whilst I was with them that I got the offer of a free all-expenses paid trips to South Africa. The catch was we had to do some pretty challenging boat races. This was during the apartheid era. The Apartheid (1948 to 1994) in South Africa was the racial segregation under the all-white government of South Africa which dictated that non-white South Africans (a majority of the population) were required to live in separate areas from whites and use separate public facilities and contact between the two groups would be limited. The different racial groups were physically separated according to their location, public facilities and social life. This got them banned from world sports so what South Africa did was host their own events. The offer of free tickets to South Africa was firstly given to two RAF guys who were in the same British Sub Aqua club as me. Fortunately, after they had been given the brief and showed the video of what was expected, they refused to participate. The owner of the club, knowing I was a former Royal Marine and thought my resolve would be stronger, offered the place to me provided

I could find another companion. As you can imagine, a free ticket to South Africa every year was a temptation that my friend Tony, also a former Royal Marine and on HMS Endurance with me, just could not resist. So after talking with my boss I got the time off work to start the trips. Our sponsor for our trips was a gentleman who owned a large company called Natal Earth Works and he predominantly did tarmac roads. He was in touch with another company here in the UK and was hoping to expand into exporting bespoke furniture from South Africa. The challenges, however, were not easy. We were competing with teams from South Africa, Australia, New Zealand, France, Spain, Italy and Germany. Obviously, this was all black market sports events because of the ban in place. The sport was racing inflatable boats such as Zodiacs and Geminis, three days to travel inland then race down the Umgeni river which is full of waterfalls and rocks and shallow areas.

The Umgeni River or Mgeni River(Zulu: uMngeni) is a river in KwaZulu-Natal, South Africa. It rises in the "Dargle" in the KZN Midlands, and its mouth is at Durban, some distance north of Durban's natural harbour. It is generally agreed its name means "the river of entrance" in Zulu, though other meanings have been suggested. The river is approximately 232 kilometres (144 miles) long with a catchment area of 4,432 square kilometres (1,711 sq mi). The Howick Falls are some famous waterfalls on the Mngeni. These were part of the negotiations needed when racing. Avoiding going through them. Once everyone had finished the first stage, we would then start the second stage which was done in the open waters of the Indian Ocean. The race in open water was at a very choppy area well known for its high surf. The challenge was getting out without being tipped over by the crashing waves. The boat had foot holding straps so you could slide your foot in to prevent you being catapulted into the air. Tony was at the rear on the engine and throttle arm and I was up front as ballast to try and keep the nose of the boat down as we were smashed by the waves and thrown around like a cork. I remember on the first day of the open water race we had to get out through the massive surf then a bit of a slalom round several buoys to the finish line. We had just managed to get away from the shore and started our slalom when we got hit by a huge wave which threw me out of the boat and into the surf. It was so scary as you could not see the boats coming, only hear the scream of the engines as the props were lifted out of the water. It was to my embarrassment that one of the South African boats was an all-woman team and they grabbed me out of the water and dropped me ashore before continuing out to the race again. That evening we had a big barbecue, or as the South Africans call it a braai. The "braaievleis", the South African version of the barbecue, comes from the combination of the Afrikaans words "braai" meaning "to grill" and "vleis" meaning "meat". Braaievleis, therefore, means "grilled meat". But you can imagine the grilling I got being a former British Royal Marine being lifted out of the water by South African girls. They certainly made a meal of it that night.

We had two good years of racing until our sponsor got himself killed. He had secured a large job in Johannesburg and brought his own people from Durban to do the work. He was approached by local blacks and told if he works in Johannesburg he must use local people. His answer was quite simply no, I use who I want to use. Next time he flew in with his helicopter they shot him. That was the end of our trips. Unfortunately, when I got back to the UK after that trip I received a phone call from my boss's wife explaining that I was no longer working with the company, and I was to return the car once I got home. Turns out that because I had supported her during some tough times she went through with her husband, who did not treat her with respect, and I managed to find her accommodation and tried to get her to go to social services, I was sacked. When I drove into work on Monday to hand everything back all the electricians pulled me to one side and expressed that they would all rather come with me, so if I was setting up on my own again to call them.

To my surprise I also received a call from a company who I had just priced a big job for. The owner fortunately heard through the grapevine what had happened and gave me the heads up on what was needed to win the contract. This was music to my ears because the new factory unit I had just won the contract for was right outside the front door of my now old boss's works office. You can imagine the glee on my face having been sacked one week and the next employing most of his electricians wiring the factory unit he thought he had won the contract for. Divine justice, I thought to myself.

It wasn't long after this that I received a phone call from Tony claiming I owed him a favour, being that he had helped me with the South African races. He wanted to do the Three Peaks Challenge in 24 hours and needed a driver. The National Three Peaks Challenge is a demanding adventure that involves climbing the highest peaks in Scotland (Ben Nevis), England (Scafell Pike), and Wales (Snowdon) within a set timeframe. You can tackle it in 24 hours or over three days, covering a total ascent of 3,000 metres and 23 miles. It's the ultimate test of endurance, perfect for those looking to push their limits and experience the UK's stunning landscapes. Of course, Tony and two of his colleagues wanted to do it in 24 hours. They wanted me to do the driving. So, I agreed and I set off from Plymouth by car to pick them up from Preston then onwards to Ben Nevis. Ben Nevis stands at the western end of the Grampian Mountains in the Highland region of Lochaber, close to the town of Fort William. A beautiful part of the world. We stayed overnight and waited till morning to start the challenge. I decided I wasn't going to hang around waiting for them each time so joined in the fun. So off we went, another massive challenge to endure. I won't say it was easy, doing the three peaks was not so bad for me but all the driving was difficult, especially to get it all done in 24 hours. I was pretty well done by the end of Snowdon in Wales. It wasn't so bad for the lads as they took turns in keeping me talking as the others slept. For me it was 24 hours with no sleep and all physical. But hey, another unexpected adventure ticked off a non-existent list.

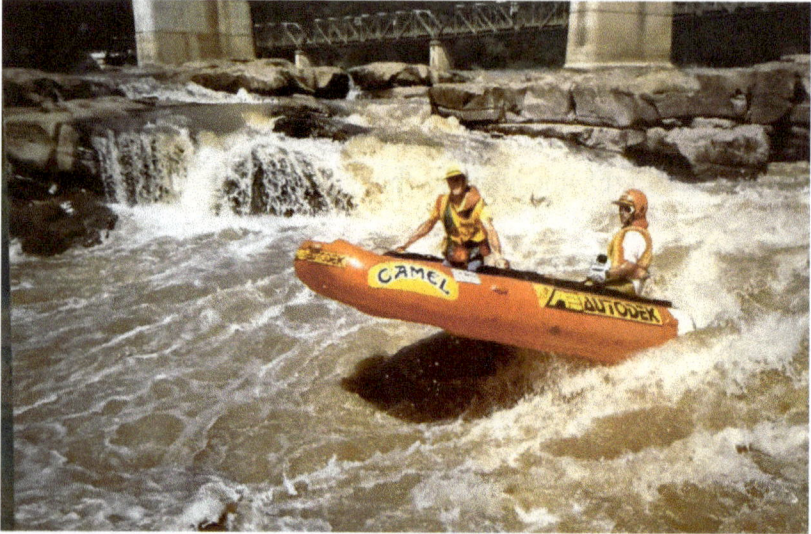

Figure 44 Durban River Race

Figure 45 Bumpy Ride

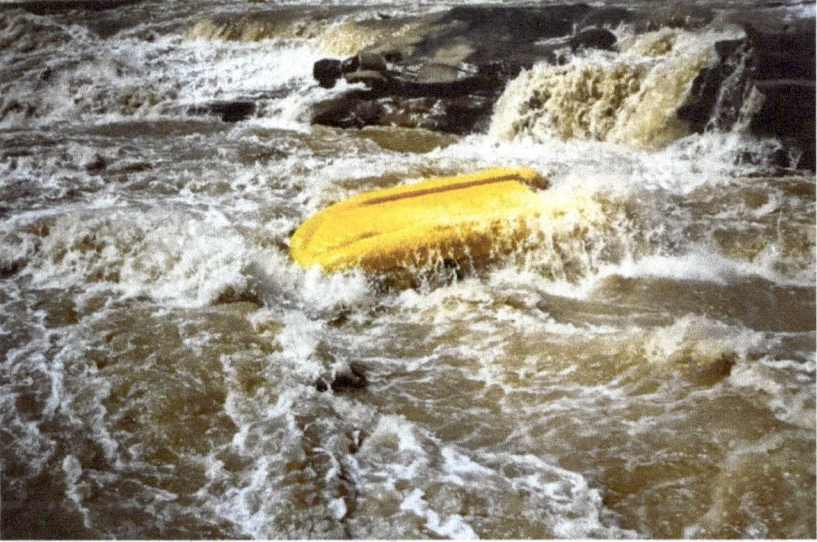

Figure 46 Oops someone didn't make it

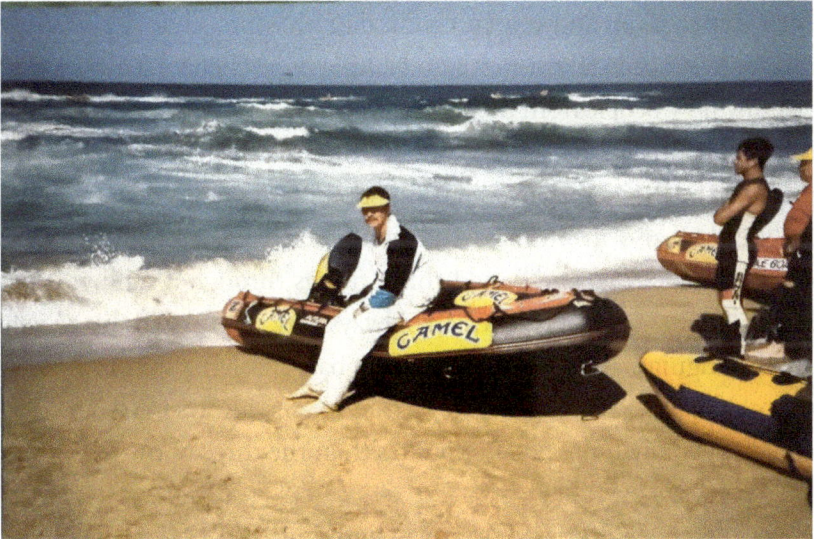

Figure 47 Really, we have to go out in that

My business was now doing very well, that first push and the large industrial unit to wire put me on a good footing. My brother Malcolm worked with me, and he finished off his apprenticeship by going to day release college. A good shout otherwise who knows where he would be now. Probably still in a pot wash. I managed to buy my first house. It's always difficult to get your foot in the housing market but work was going well which gave me the income to get a mortgage. The property I bought was a rundown house and I managed to get planning permission to turn it into two flats. I sold the top flat and I lived in the bottom flat for a while. I later got my brother onto the housing market as the business had picked up a bit more. I managed to secure a mortgage for him, and he moved into my flat. I then moved to a house. I recall he almost changed his mind mid-way through. I had already committed to the house purchase and as you couldn't have two mortgages it was reliant on the flat sale. Fortunately, he saw sense and completed the purchase. I think this was the start of his housing investments. He didn't see it at the time but getting on the housing market was always difficult and this got him there. Malcolm has always been very cautious and very methodical in his approach to life, whereas I have always been adventurous and taking huge chances. I always find it funny how people from the same family and blood line can take such different approaches through life. There was me always taking chances, pushing the limits, I enjoyed pushing boundaries not only in my own abilities but also in business and lifestyle. Yet Malcolm was always cautious, indecisive and would think things through a million times and still not come to a conclusion. Always very careful with his money and belongings, always looking for that bargain. My sister Angela, on the other hand, was rebellious, very carefree and always in trouble. You couldn't get any more polar opposites than the three of us.

It was October 30th 1994, I was living at 369 Old Laira Road, Plymouth when my mobile rang. It was my cousin Dave. Hey Al, I have some bad news for you, I'm sorry to say but your mother was found dead yesterday; it would appear to be an overdose. Well, I've been around death a lot through my life's experiences, but this floored me. I had had a long conversation with her the night before. We talked about so many things, she even expressed an interest in me taking her family name, which at the time was strange but in hindsight I can see what she was angling at. She had been prescribed Co-Proxamol and unfortunately taken too many. Co-Proxamol is taken for mild to moderate pain. In 2007 the medicines and healthcare products regulatory agency (MHRA) stopped the licence for Co-proxamol because of safety concerns. The lethal dose of Co-proxamol is quite low and it is even more lethal if taken with alcohol or other drugs. I've had many a conversation about the subject of suicide. Both with friends and family. A lot of people think suicide is mainly a mental health issue. Whilst this might be true in some cases, I personally do not believe it true in my mother's case. Most of my family preferred that I did not refer to my mother's death as suicide, and just to say she died. The difference of somebody just dying and of somebody committing suicide has a hugely different effect on others left behind. For example, dying of natural causes or being killed accidentally does not raise the same questions as somebody taking their own life. When someone dies of natural causes or is killed accidentally, whilst still tragic, it is grieved in a different way. You are saddened by the occurrence, either they had a long and enjoyable life and it was time, or it's unfortunate they were in the wrong place at the wrong time, and you mourn their passing; but when it's suicidal it brings together a more questionable grieving. Could I have done something more, why didn't I read the signs better, did I do enough? The grieving has more of a questionable guilt with it and in turn affects you in a different way. Many think that people who commit suicide are not in a sane state of mind and hence refer to it as a mental health issue. That's not always the case. My mother was a very proud woman and very strong in character. When my parents divorced, my mother was persuaded to move up to the Isle of Lewis to a place called Breasclete. Breasclete (Scottish Gaelic: Brèascleit) is a village and community on the west side of the Isle of Lewis, in the Outer Hebrides, Scotland. Breasclete is within the parish of Uig, and is situated adjacent to the A858. It's a very desolate area but she wanted to be close to her sister. Unfortunately, her sister was married to a very controlling husband, and it wasn't long before my mother found herself isolated in the middle of nowhere. Her sister was stopped from visiting her and Breasclete is not exactly populated – when my mother lived there the population was 68 – I think today it is 107, so not the place to be alone in. On the move from Spalding in Lincolnshire to the Isle of Lewis most of my mother's furniture was damaged and this did not help matters. She was living in a cold house with very minimal furniture. Not something she was accustomed to, having come from a far better lifestyle in the services. It took about two years plus to fight the matter in court and unfortunately as the removal company was from the Isle of Lewis she didn't have much chance of winning. Life became very hard with no work and living in a remote rural location with little to no contact with family. Years of this took its toll and she made a command decision to end it all. To understand her decision, you have to put yourself in her shoes. In her mind her family had their own lives to live, all very busy. She did not want to be a burden on anyone and felt that with her out of the way we could live our life without worrying about her, plus she could leave a little something to us all from the proceeds of the sale of her house. She had had enough of difficult times and was at peace with her decision. With this well thought through, and carefully calculated, she made her farewell calls to us all, left us little gifts and called it a day. This was not the mind of a mental disorder, but a calculated decision based on circumstances and a strong will that enough is enough. I find people are quick in judgment when it comes to suicidal acts without understanding the person's reasons. They say there is help out there for people who feel this urge. Is there really? I have questioned this myself. Yes, we have the Samaritans and other such services that are around to talk to people who feel down and suicidal, but that's it. It's the kind of talk that says, that's ok, my lovely, things will look better in the morning. Which, don't get me wrong, it's a fantastic service for people who are momentarily depressed. What about those who have really no way out, who genuinely can't better their situation and who genuinely believe it's time to go and don't want to be a burden on others? All the talk in the world won't change their mind. And dare I say it, it's not in my view a mental illness but more a calculated decision.

Because my parents had divorced the whole organisation of the death fell to me being the eldest. There was so much to think about and organise. I almost felt I didn't have time to grieve with all the phone calls and house selling arrangements, the funeral, who carried the coffin when to empty the house etc. I will always remember going up to the house with my brothers and sister. It was the most difficult time of my life. Trying to remain strong for them. I remember we all stayed together in the same room. I recall going out by myself when the others were sleeping to let out some emotions in private and so as not to upset the others. We were there to bag everything up and square everything away. It was a very difficult time for us all. We were also given time in private to say our goodbyes to my mother as she lay in the coffin. I recall putting my picture beside her and my military medals which she had never seen. To this day I don't know why I did that but at the time it felt right that I was giving her something very personal to me to have by her side. I always felt I should have been there more for her instead of always being away. I guess my lifestyle was always such that I travelled and seldom stayed in one place long enough to have her stay with me. All these things go through your head at a time like this. All the if-only questions. I have done many things in my life and to date I have no regrets apart from the one thing which always haunts me. I could have done more for her. If only.

I did change my name, though after some research a friend of mine made the connection between Sheldrake and McCloud. I chose McCloud.

* * *

CHAPTER 12

I continued running my own business and by now had several guys working with me. We had become quite a reputable company and were doing quite well despite the construction industry being in a bad period. The construction industry had not been in such a bad way since the 1930s and the suggestions were it would not climb its way out of decline until at least 1996. To keep the guys going I managed to find work in London, so we had half the guys working in London with the other half covering the South West. It was a difficult time, and I had several companies go bankrupt on me which caused even more strain on my finances. It was during this time I received a call from a colleague of mine, a former Royal Marine who asked if I would be interested in a job in Algeria. At first, I thought he was taking the mick but it soon became apparent it was a genuine offer. He was doing security for BP who were in the process of building a base camp but needed more electricians. The job was located in a place called Hassi Messaoud.

Hassi Messaoud is a town in Ouargla Province, eastern Algeria, located 85 kilometres (53 mi) southeast of Ouargla. As of 2008 it had a population of 45,147 people, up from 40,360 in 1998, and an annual population growth rate of 1.1%, the lowest in the province. Oil was discovered there in 1956, and the town's prominence has grown rapidly since then; it is considered as the First Energy town in

Algeria where all the big oil and gas companies have offices and bases. It is an oil refinery town named after the first oil well. A water well, dug in 1917, can be found on the airport side of town. Today there are over 800 wells within a 25 kilometres (16 mi) radius of the town. The job entailed wiring up prefabricated buildings once they had been built. It was only for three weeks, but as business was slow, we took up the offer. So, my brother Malcolm and I went over. Because we were still in the mind-set that time is money we were cracking out the units quite quickly, so much so that in the end the construction company had got rid of all the other electricians and ended up keeping myself and my brother to the end. So, what was supposed to be a three-week job ended up being a 13-week assignment. BP were moving in for Christmas and were desperate to complete the recreation room and bar by then. We successfully managed to complete this and as it was now the end of the contract, BP put on a large barbecue party for us as a way of saying thank you. The BP project manager for the Algeria assignment flew in to open the base. It was during this time when I was at the bar chatting to the lads that the BP boss came over to see me. I understand you're a dive instructor? he asked me. Yes, I replied. Well in that case how would you like to stay on here? I would like to be the first British Sub Aqua club in the Sahara desert but to do that I need a dive instructor. Sounds fun, I said, but what job am I going to do? Don't worry about a job, he answered. I will find a position for you, and that's how I ended up working in oil and gas.

He got me set up through an agency working as the maintenance manager for the base we had just built, and I in turn got my brother over as one of the maintenance guys. I slowly dissolved the company in the UK and focused on my new position in Algeria.

The Algeria project manager had a special pool built and shipped over 12 sets of diving equipment and a compressor to enable the filling of the cylinders. I used to take people who were interested through the BSAC courses. We could do all the training and all the pool work, but in order to become a sport diver you had to do two open water dives before I could sign off the logbook, so once we got people up to standard we would fly over to Egypt, courtesy of BP and complete the open water tests giving them a diving qualification. My rotation at this time was six weeks on two weeks off, although this is quite a difficult rotation. We were in the middle of the Sahara Desert with temperatures climbing as high as 50C in the summer so always had a great tan with money in the bank and nowhere to spend it. The bar was free so was all our food and accommodation, so life was quite good. I used to organise sporting events and quizzes etc. I decorated the bar, and we ended up with a great atmosphere considering we were at work. Although this was considered a hardship posting for BP employees, it was in fact more like a holiday camp.

Every year I would organise a big Hassi Messaoud It's a knockout sporting event. This would consist of teams competing through various silly games. It was based on the TV It's a knockout competition and was a great team building event and loads of fun. Although this was the fun side there was also a serious side. Part of my job was to build up a strong maintenance team, preferably using local engineers. This is always a complex task in third world countries because qualifications and education are few and far between. More so in such a small catchment area. I developed some basic tests to put the guys through and it wasn't long before I had a well-oiled team who were keen to advance and learn. Hassi was now BP's headquarters; it was a joint venture with the Algerian state oil and gas company Sonatrach. We were starting to do a lot of seismic operations in the search for more gas wells to exploit. We soon had another little area called Tiguentourine to start drilling in. This was about an hour and 20 minutes' flight in a small Beech aircraft. We first had to establish a base camp. So, I took advantage of this to get a couple of my electricians over to build and wire the prefab buildings. We built a small canteen and recreation room together with four six-man accommodation blocks. The base was run off two generators for power. Once finished, my brother and one of the other electricians, Adrian, were based there to look after the place. With the increase in finding more gas pockets came the requirement for more men and consequently we had to increase the size of our headquarters at Hassi Messaoud. Because I was instrumental in building the base, I was tasked with its extension and so designed and installed the extra accommodation and infrastructure required. Once all the drilling had taken place and everything was capped ready for production, there was a bit of downtime. During this period Hassi was down to a skeleton crew of a few office workers in finance, security and maintenance staff just looking after the base. Tiguentourine was also closed down, the generators silenced and the camp derelict.

During this downtime, I was poached by a local company run by two Algerian brothers Riad and Madjid, they used to provide logistics and drivers etc to BP during the project. They wanted to build a base camp much like BP's to house oil workers. It was a smart move as they could see the expansion of Hassi within oil and gas and the need for facilities. They were probably the equivalent to the Kray twins back in the days. Nothing happened in Hassi without their knowledge and say-so. I recall many times coming in from Gatwick on the charter flight with loads of equipment. As soon as I walked down the stairs off the flight I was collected on the runway. My passport was taken by the brothers' contacts. I didn't go through customs at all but drove straight to the base in a Landcruiser together with all the materials, and my passport would appear later in the day with all the necessary stamps and permissions on. It felt like something out of a spy movie. Needless to say, we got the camp built and ready for the return of various companies returning now having gone from exploration to the development stage.

I was soon back with BP and ready to start again. I will always remember with fond memories the reopening of Tiguentourine. Myself and one security guy were flown out to the base; we were there to get the place ready for occupants. The two of us were chosen to go because the security guy was ex-French Foreign Legion and I of course ex-Royal Marines, so we were both happy with being in remote places alone. We needed to service the generators and get them up and running, having been left dormant for some 12 months. My first job was to get one of them up and running so we at least had power to start. It took me two days to get the generator up and running, by the time I charged the batteries and swapped out a few other items, tested and completed all the pre-checks, but once we had power we were in a good place. Once the generator had been run for a little time, I switched it over to send power, then went around all the rooms checking everything was functioning. My colleague came to see me and asked if I had any washing to be done. We both had two days of washing so he said he would get that done whilst I continued to test everything. What I didn't expect was for him to put new red towels in with the washing load. Yep, for the rest of our trip we had pink clothing. I don't need to tell you what the rest of the security, all ex-SAS, Royal Marines and French Foreign Legion boys said; needless to say they had enough ammunition for months to come. Not only that but they had photos of us coming back, him in pink camouflage clothes and me in pink work clothes.

It took a while to get back to normal and for the comments to subside, but life was becoming busy now the development of getting the gas out was full on and more and more people were using the base.

With a greater number of people joining the base the gym was no longer just used for the few, but we now had to cater for a lot more. As a result, more health and safety was showing its face. This meant we now couldn't just let anyone in the gym; they had to have a gym induction and be shown how to use the equipment correctly. So, myself and a few of the security boys, all ex SAS, Legion and Marines were sent back to the UK to do a gym instructors' course. This was a good number for us because it was just a ticking the box exercise being that we were all still physically active and always used the gym anyway. I used to still do a lot of running and I recall one afternoon walking through the finance office when one of the BP accountants called out, asking me if I had watched the Eurosports channel last night, it was all about the Marathon des Sables.

Marathon des Sables, or MdS, (French for Marathon of the Sands) is a seven-day, about 257km (160 miles) ultramarathon, which is approximately the distance of six regular marathons. The longest single stage was 91km (57 miles) long. This is run as a double marathon through the night. This multi-day race is held every year in southern Morocco, in the Sahara Desert. Some runners regard it as one of the toughest foot races on Earth. Anyway, I recall saying "yes I watched it, I bet that's a tough race". There was no mention of, I want to do it. Yet when the security boys came into the bar that night (one SAS, three French Foreign Legion) they said, hey Al we hear you're doing the Marathon des Sables. I just laughed and said yeah really. That was enough to start the banter about how Marines could never accomplish such a task etc. Okay yes, I did take the bait, but I did say, I will do it if you do. So, the agreement was made that we would do the run together. We had about three months to train for it so plenty of time, also the fact we were already in the Sahara Desert the training was first hand. Or so I thought. We contacted the organisers, and it wasn't long before we had our information pack. Within the pack it gave you a list of items you had to have with you. The race is over seven days, and you have to be self-sufficient. There were obligatory items you had to have such as:

- A WAA Ultra Bag 20L backpack or equivalent
- A packaging capacity of 1.5 litres of water (gourd, water bag, etc.)
- A sleeping bag
- A headlamp (which must be turned on after dark) + 1 complete set of spare batteries or battery
- 10 safety pins
- A lighter
- A whistle
- A compass
- A metal blade knife
- A skin antiseptic
- A signalling mirror
- A survival blanket
- Flares
- 8 soup cubes to help the rehydration
- A tube of sunscreen
- 100 euros in cash
- Passport or identity card
- The official MDS medical certificate completed by a doctor
- A race kit is also provided by the organization and given during the technical and medical checks, which contain:
- The bibs
- a front bib (upper part of the chest)
- a back bib (on the backpack)
- The roadbook
- The road book is the MDS runner's guide, in which you will find all the information concerning the adventure:
- A route map

- Details concerning the stages (programme, map, terrain, etc.)
- The table of penalties.

These were the basics you had to carry; on top of this you must have your food to last the seven days. Any personal medical additions. Spare clothing etc. All your stuff was marked with permanent marker pen and anything found or littered would cost penalty points against you. If you were caught with any missing items, you would be disqualified. At the start of each race a handful of random numbers would be picked and the contents of the pack examined. Water checkpoints were at various stages of the race, so you had to make sure you controlled your water intake so as not to run out before a checkpoint. This was quite difficult particularly as the summer heat in the Sahara can get well above 40C. At the end of each day the Bedouin trackers would set up lean-to tents for you to overnight. This is when you would cook your food and tend to any injury you might have picked up. So, we were set and we had three months to train. But guess what. Everyone dropped out before the start date with various excuses. In the end out of all the tough talkers the only two who attended the race were myself and my brother. SAS, Legion, French special forces. Really, nowhere to be seen. They're very good at talking the talk but not at walking the talk. As you can imagine, I had great joy letting them know once again not only are they trained by Royal Marines they are outdone by Royal Marines. One of my mistakes when starting the race was not listening to the advice that was given about footwear – the advice was to get footwear two sizes too big which because we were training in the Sahara anyway I deemed as not necessary. However, after the first day my feet were very badly blistered. Fortunately for me, Automatic who was an ex-Navy medic, gave me some pretty powerful painkillers. I think without those I might not have reached the end of the race. It was ironic that on the second day of the race we had a mail call. Unbeknown to me because the race is world-renowned it is always shown on Eurosport, and colleagues and family could follow your progress. So, you can imagine my surprise when my name got called out as having received messages. My brother looked at me as if to say who is messaging you, Allen. It was only the security boys and all of Hassi base who were following the race. The message simply read: well done so far, Royal, but if you don't finish, don't come back. My feet were already in bits but with a message like that there was no way I was not going to finish. The race gets harder day by day and one of our days was through a sandstorm which didn't help at all. Also, one of the days is a dune day. This was running on pure soft sand which if you have cuts and blisters can be quite nasty. Fortunately, we had brought with us some gators to prevent the Sand getting into our running shoes. Infection could quickly set in, especially with no showers en route. I just carried wet wipes so each day I could at least clean myself to a degree each evening. I used to sleep with my feet resting over a water bottle so as not to touch the ground, the pain from the blisters was so intense. Putting my running shoes on each morning was nothing short of torture. On the double marathon day you have a choice: you can either run through the night, thereby getting the following day free, or you can stop after halfway and then continue the following day with no free rest day. We chose to run through the night as did many others. Navigation at night is a lot harder and I recall getting to the top of one of the dunes and most runners seemed to be heading to my left, which for some reason didn't sit right with me. I asked my brother to get my sketch map out of my pack from my back and orientated myself with the compass. By my reckoning, we should be going slightly right; my brother being a bit unsure questioned me, particularly as everyone else was going slightly left. It had been a hard day, and I did not want mistakes adding to my journey so I said I was following my instinct. It wasn't long until we looked behind us to see that everyone else had started following us, which was actually a good thing because we were heading in the right direction. The organisers had a beacon of light showing the end point for that day; it was still somewhere in the distance and my brother was feeling a lot better than I was so decided to run ahead. He said he would get the food on for when I got to the tent. The ground was very rocky and undulating by now and I recall running down a rather steep decline and almost falling over one of the other contestants. It was an Italian man, and he was almost in tears. He had given up. He kept kicking stones because his torch had died, and he had no batteries left so could not find his way. I had a head torch and persuaded him to run slowly with me and I would get him to the finish line. The camaraderie of people in the race is amazing as everyone always tries to help everyone else. The following morning, he managed to find me and could not thank me enough. He gave me a handful of energy drinks as a way of saying thank you, and boy did I need them for the next stage. I've done a lot of challenging events in my time, but this was up there as one of the hardest. At the end of each day's racing the lean-to tent you share, you share with the same people all the time, so we were kind of a group. Unbeknown to everyone, my brother and I had each carried a miniature half bottle of red wine which we got from the hotel on the first day, we had carried it throughout the race specifically for this point in the race. When we pulled the bottles from our packs to share with the tent and wish everyone the best of luck for the final run, it went down really well. That final run, although not quite as long as the others, was extremely exhausting and passing through the finish line when they hang the medal around your neck is one of the best feelings ever. When we got back to the hotel and into our room, I had to physically cut my running shoes off my feet. My feet were so swollen and sore. It took me almost a week to walk normally again. It was another experience added to my lifetime achievements and although I was coaxed into it, I did enjoy it and once again when I got back to Algeria, it was my turn to tease.

Figure 48 Start of MDS

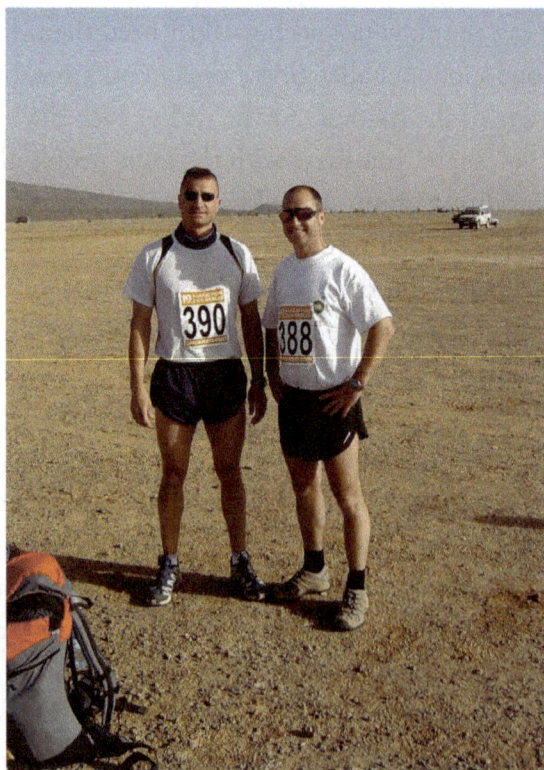

Figure 49 Brother and I ready to go

Figure 50 First Checkpoint in site marathon 1 done.

Figure 51 Ouch and only day one.

Figure 52 The pain showing through

Figure 53 End of day makeshift cover

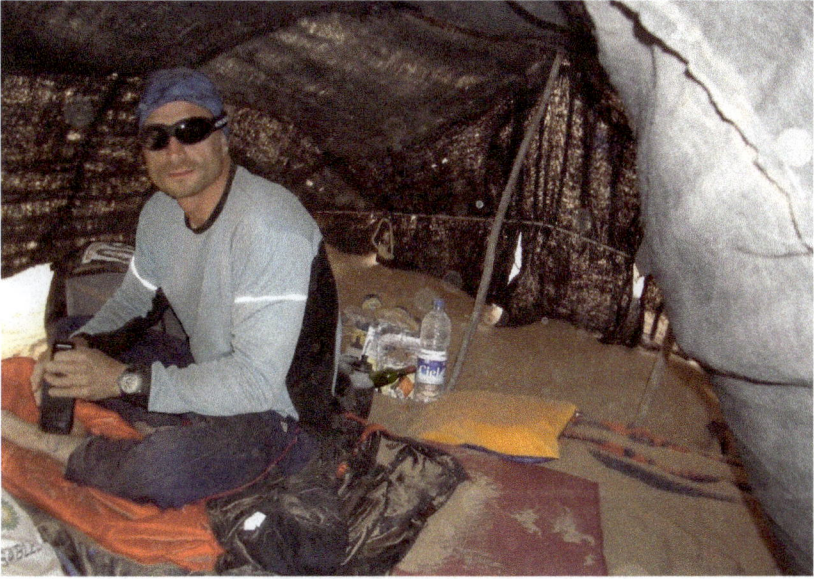

Figure 54 Brother inside shelter, day's run done

Figure 55 Dune Day

Figure 56 Start of Dune day

Figure 57 Running on such fine sand

Figure 58 Brother and I finally over the dunes

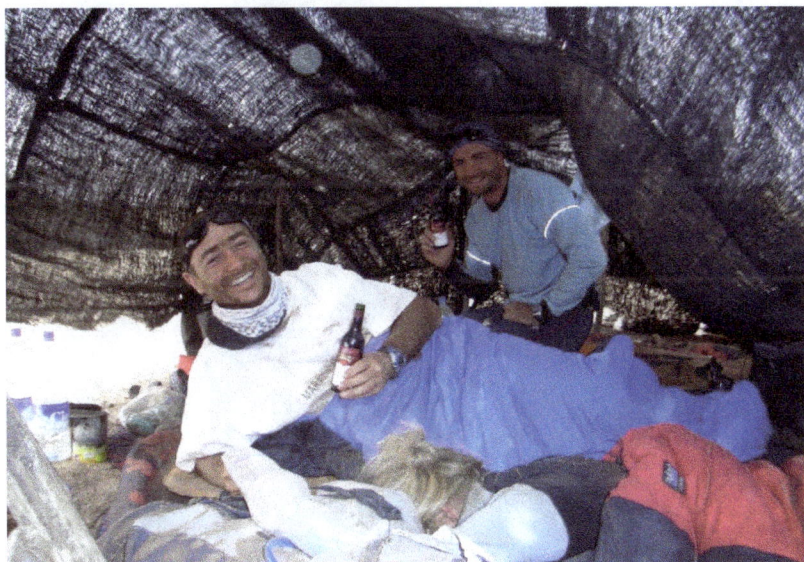

Figure 59 Yes, brother and I carried the bottles of wine everyday
just to celebrate our last night in shelters.

Figure 60 Finish Line

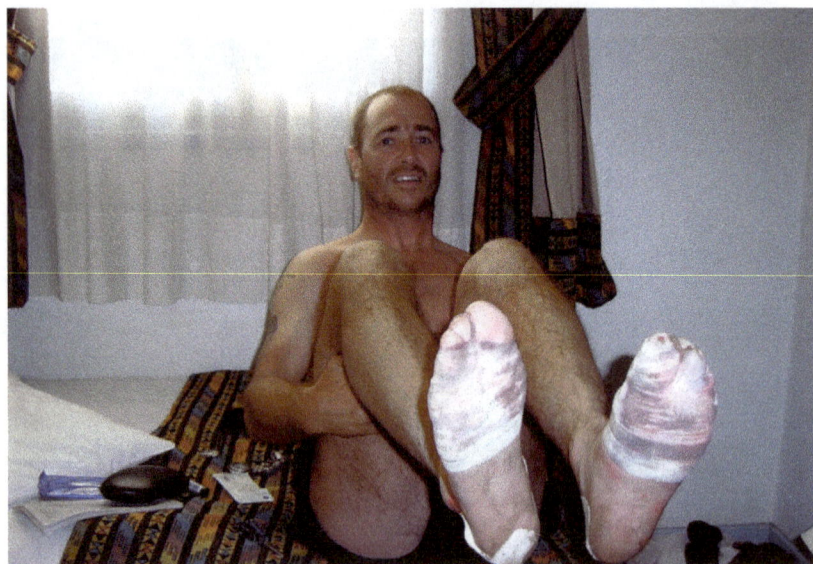

Figure 61 Cut off trainers

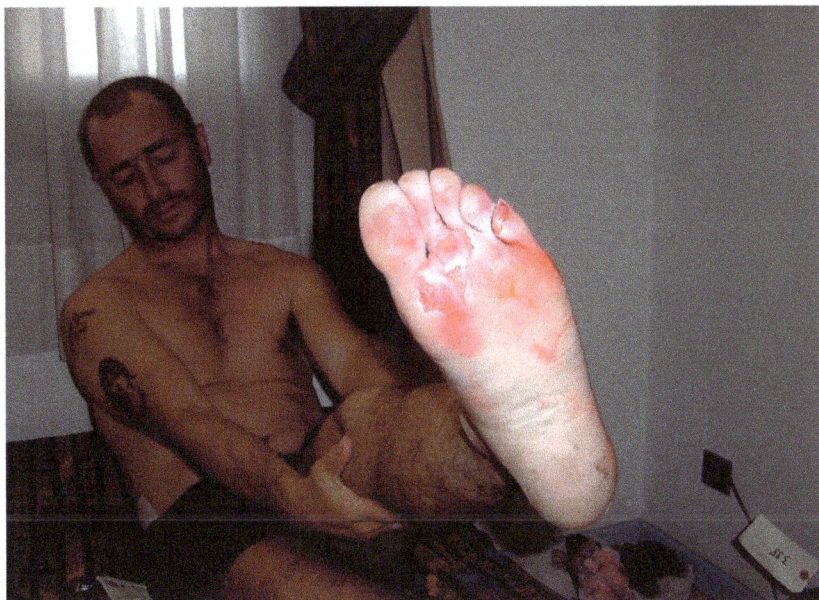

Figure 62End of race pain

BP had now sold a lot of their shares to Statoil, Norway's oil and gas company. This now had become a three-way joint venture which as you can imagine has its difficulties. It was once again time to extend the base. We had a large influx of local Sonatrach personnel and Statoil personnel. As a consequence, we needed a lot more accommodation, a bigger kitchen and dining room, and a larger recreational area, so the next base extension was quite substantial. Once again, I was tasked with the electrical design and installation and also the positioning layout of the new buildings. It was a Turkish company that had won the bidding contract and one of my jobs was to go over to Turkey and check the build quality of the units. So, I flew over to Ankara and was wined and dined by the Turkish contractors. It was more like a holiday than a task.

✳ ✳ ✳

CHAPTER 13

❧

My rotation had changed, and I was now doing three weeks on and three weeks off. This was particularly good for going on holidays. It was during one of my times off when a well-known pub in Plymouth that we used to frequent a lot came up for sale. After a lot of consideration, I thought it would be a good investment and could end up a nice little money pump if I bought it and had a manager run it. I discussed this with my brother and another friend of mine who I was in the Marines with. I thought it would be good for them as an investment too. It was a freehold pub with a 25-year lease. It was located in the busiest part of the Barbican. I discussed it with a very well-known bar lady who had a vast experience in the trade. She agreed she would run it for me, and I just wanted to be the silent owner. We bought the lease and refurbished the bar and things were looking good. Well, they were until the downturn of the pub industry. Things started to get a little harder to survive. I was constantly having to input money to keep it afloat. My brother and my friend were not really around much. My brother was living in Belgium, and my friend didn't really show much interest despite the investment they had contributed. Things were always left to me. My girlfriend at the time was an accountant for BP. She used to do the accounts for the pub. After some discussions about the finances, I decided I should try and recoup some of my investment. I had put considerably more than the others into the project. Obviously at the time working in oil and gas I was in a position to do this – they weren't. However, I did want it returned. After discussions with the accountant, I decided to take out various amounts as and when I could to try and get back to an even investment, so all three of us had the same level of investment. This, however, was proving difficult. I was constantly away and found it difficult to keep a tight grip on the pub. The stress caused lots of arguments between my brother and my friend and myself. In the end, I told them I had had enough, and they could take a turn at running it or lose it. All this time they had shown very little interest but now things were difficult and there was a possibility we could lose it, suddenly they were interested. I handed everything over to them and asked the accountant to give them all the books and let them have a crack at reviving it. It was during this time that they went through the books and then accused me of taking money out saying this was the reason for the downturn. As you can imagine, I was not too happy. I told them to look at the amount I'd put in and that what I was taking out I was entitled to. Obviously, they saw it differently. This was the start of a large fallout with my brother. I don't think we talked much after that, probably about three years before we even became slightly sociable again. Once again there was a clear divide on views. I am happy taking chances, him forever the cautious. It was all sweet when they thought they could perhaps make some money but hey when it didn't go to plan it all got nasty. In the end, however, when they realised it wasn't to be, it was left to me to try and get rid of the pub. Fortunately, the landlady liked me, and she took it back off my hands. It wasn't long after that that she sold the building completely simply because the pub industry had gone. Unfortunately, we had lost our investment. But for me, I just thought nothing ventured, nothing gained. I'm not really all that materialistic, I enjoy the adventure more than the reward. I wish I could say the same for my friend and brother. It's funny how some people love to be involved if there's a possible gain, but when it doesn't go to plan, quickly look to apportion blame. It's not like people invest to lose, so why all the noise. Far better to dust yourself down and carry on. It's not the end of the world.

I took quite a hit on that adventure, losing over £60,000.00 which was not great. Not long after falling out with my brother, I received a phone call from a close colleague of mine. He was ex-South African special forces, he'd got into a bit of trouble and had to get out of South Africa for a while so ended up joining the French Foreign Legion. He spent 12 years with the Legion which by all accounts is impressive. When I met him, he was doing security for BP in Algeria. Although his French was extremely good, he still had his South African twang and spoke very good Afrikaans. On the call he asked how I was doing and was sorry to hear I had fallen out with my brother whom he also knew quite well. I'll cut to the chase, he said, how would you like to make some of that money back? I'm all ears, I said. I'm in London at the end of the month. Let's meet in the Albannach bar and I'll fill you in with the details. He, like me, loved his whisky and Albannach is a truly unique venue, presenting the best of Scotland with an unrivalled range of Scottish Malts, in excess of 120, and a menu using only the best produce from north of the border. We found a seat upstairs and ordered a good old Haggis with mashed potatoes and we sat drinking fine malts as he filled me in on the job details.

The task was to provide an armed security guard for a number of containers arriving in the Mozambique port of Beira to be transported to Harare airport in Zimbabwe. It's not the worst part of the world, but by no means the safest either, but then I guess these types of jobs only come up in the not-so-nice areas. I was also aware that he had been involved in a great deal of mercenary works, and this felt very much along those lines. My first question was whether it is legal or illegal. He assured me it was all above board. The containment was largely food supplies, machinery and transport equipment and some miscellaneous manufactured goods. With some armaments, which I was assured was 100% above board and for delivery to the Zimbabwe Defence Industries ZDI. I have known this man for many years, and I know he would not try to pull the wool over my eyes, so I was leaning on the side of trust and had to believe he was saying it as it is. On top of that the money was quite mediocre for the task. It was R110,000.00 and it was paid in Rand. This was understandable because the rule was anything over R25,000 coming out of South Africa had to have written permission which could be problematic for the employer. So, it did all seem legitimate. After a few more whiskies I agreed to participate in the task. I adjusted my rotation so I could do the job during my three-week leave period. We flew into Harare airport in Zimbabwe and picked up three Armoured Toyota Landcruisers. These were standard security issued vehicles in the private security sector, we were a team of eight and everything was awaiting our arrival as planned. The security company had our equipment, weapons and vehicles. Although we had our own route mapping on us, we were again provided with everything needed for the journey. Because of the massive corruption in this part of the world and the number of roadblocks and hijackings, we were advised to take the offbeat route to avoid too much exposure. Our trip to the port of Beira was a form of recce. We drove the route we intended to return by so we could assess any dangerous obstacles we may encounter. It wasn't unusual to have what we call illegal vehicle checkpoints pop up run by gangs and hoodlums trying to make a quick buck. I guess that's why we were the security detail. We collected our equipment and headed for the port. Coming out of Harare the main road common to most is the A3; however, this was full of pay tolls and corrupt checkpoints. We took the A4 which avoided toll roads. Although a bumpier, rough ride in comparison, the A3 was renowned for robberies. We did occasionally use some parts of the A3 but stayed away as much as we could. We had road maps as well as satnav because it's not unheard of for a satnav to take you down a dead end which you certainly don't need with our cargo. The journey took us the best part of 15 hours so we knew it would be slower on the return, particularly with the container trucks as some of the roads were quite narrow. Going through some of the townships was also an eye opener and very scary. It was just like you see on TV, as rough as can be with extreme poverty. We waited just outside the port for our vehicles to clear customs. It took quite some time before our trucks arrived. I believe there was some bribery going on because our trucks were the last to be cleared. This was not so good because it now meant a good deal of our journey would be done at night. The return journey was slow going. The roads are not lit up like ours and you struggle to avoid potholes and stray animals. Driving, especially at night, is difficult. I will never forget this return trip; we were travelling in an extended convoy with a gap of between three and four truck lengths between us. This kept us spread over a longer distance, which in turn made it difficult to roadblock. We had three guys in the front Landcruiser, then two container trucks, then three more guys in the middle Landcruiser, followed by the other two container trucks, then the two of us bringing up the rear in the last Landcruiser. Between the Landcruisers we had Motorola radios. We were dressed in civilian dress because camouflage clothing was illegal to wear by civilians in these countries. I will always remember when we got hit. Suddenly we heard gunfire, and a contact wait out came over the radio. We immediately slammed our brakes on and stopped the vehicle. The two trucks in front of us hadn't stopped and were very soon out of sight in the dark night as they turned the corner in the road. The gunfire was brief and the guys in the middle Landcruiser called military attack! stay clear! over the radio. This didn't ring right to us and fortunately we were just outside the range of the ambush. We slammed the Landcruiser into reverse and went crashing off road and into the darkness. Bandits were one thing but to be attacked by the military was something quite different. We were very fortunate that the hit was done at a place called Mhare Bridge which was a bit of an extended S bend. Travelling in such a wide convoy had paid off as we had managed to stay clear of all the commotion. We got back on the road but headed in the opposite direction. Should we not try to help,

I asked Jurgen. No, you're here to escort not to get killed, besides you heard the call. Military ambush stay clear. We head back, take another route to the airport and call headquarters. This is exactly what we did. Our instructions were to return on the return flight as planned.

To this day I have no idea what happened or why. What I do know is we lost the three guys in the lead vehicle, and the other three were imprisoned for just under four months whilst the issue was sorted out. I was convinced there was more in those containers than we had been led to believe and with it taking so long to release the others it was questionable how legit it actually was. The problem with countries like these is they are so corrupt if you don't go through all the correct channels, you can quickly become unstuck. Fortunately, Jurgen later told me the guys were not mistreated, and it was just political corruption that delayed their release. I'm still not convinced. Anyway, I got paid, although it was in several spaced-out payments, and I returned to Algeria unharmed. Thankfully I wasn't in the lead vehicle.

Figure 63 Container trucks

Figure 64 Port of Beira

Figure 65 Harare Airport

Finally, the build project in Algeria was underway. Getting things cleared through customs in Algeria is an absolute nightmare. Bringing foreign materials into this country costs almost 100% tax so the cost of your project is virtually doubled. Then you have the nightmare of bringing in foreign labour and obtaining visas for the workers, but the project was underway at least. Unfortunately, what should've taken just over a year took almost two and a half years. Most of this down to the bureaucracy of Algerian penny-pinching.

During my time in Algeria we had formed a little social club and called it the Sahara wine club. We used to bring over some fine wines and happily indulge in nights of fine food and wine in someone's accommodation. Nothing beats fine wine and cheese in the middle of the Sahara desert. We also established a little holiday group and each of us would take turns in suggesting a place to go on holiday and organising it during one of our three weeks off periods. On this occasion, it was my friend Fergie. A New Zealand lady who now lives in Scotland with her husband Dave. They decided we would go on a Safari, a very special Safari that you could not buy from a travel agent. It was a matter of who you know. My reason for adding this to my autobiography is because this holiday was an amazing experience. We flew to Nairobi in Kenya and spent our first night in the Fairview Hotel. The Fairview Hotel is a first-class hotel with a very colonial feel to it, ideal for our first stop. Everyone bought a safari hat, and we had a lovely meal in the evening with lots of chit chat about our very special safari. We were there for a day visit and the following day we were being picked up by our travel guides. Whilst we were here, we took the opportunity to visit the David Sheldrick Wildlife Trust nursery, a rescue and rehab centre for orphaned elephants, open to the public for viewing mud baths and feedings.

The Sheldrick Wildlife Trust (SWT) operates the most successful orphan elephant rescue and rehabilitation programme in the world. A couple of the team adopted a baby elephant which is quite nice as you pay a contribution towards its keep, and you get an update and videos on how it's doing. The nursery also has rhinos which it looks after.

The following day we were taken to a small airstrip to get our small Pilatus single engine aircraft just for our group to fly us to the Lewa Downs. The Lewa Wildlife Conservancy (also known as Lewa Downs) is located in northern Kenya. It was formed in 1995 and is a wildlife sanctuary which together with the adjacent Ngare Ndare Forest covers over 62,000 acres (250 km2). The Conservancy is home to a wide variety of wildlife including the rare and endangered black rhinos, Grevy's zebras and sitatungas. It also includes the big five (lion, leopards, elephants, rhinos and Cape buffaloes). Lewa holds over 12% of Kenya's eastern black rhinoceros population and the largest single population of Grevy's zebras in the world (approximately 350 individuals). Our time here as you can imagine was second to none. Everyday brought something inspiring and beautiful. It was living in the wild with your home comforts. Our next stop was Sirikoi Lodge run by Willie and Sue Roberts, in fact built by Willie and Sue Roberts, second generation Kenyans and conservationists. Sirikoi comprises a main lodge, a three-bedroom house, two-bedroom cottage, each crowned by an imposing thatched roof, and four tents facing a watering hole, for great armchair game viewing. The game just freely walks about, and it gives you the feeling of being at one with nature, never knowing what might stroll past your front entrance. Set by a natural spring on a 28 square kilometre private section of the Lewa Wildlife Conservancy area of northern Kenya, Lewa Sirikoi Lodge is an intimate and high-quality place with an abundance of wildlife freely grazing and drinking from the spring. The accommodation here was lush. The guest book had names like Diana Ross, Harrison Ford and George Michael just to name a few. Our guides for our daytime outings were superior Masai Mara tribesmen; their tracking skills were amazing. It was whilst we were here that we had a live walk into the wilderness with no vehicles. The guys were training their dogs' bloodhounds in the art of tracking. Early in the morning at sunrise we got up to do our track into the wild. The guys took a handkerchief off one of us for the dog to get the scent then returned it to us prior to setting off. We had one armed guard at the rear and one at the front and we walked in a loose single file into the unknown. Our walk was around two hours, and it certainly had the adrenaline going. My experience with bears in Canada and huge lion seals and whales in the Antarctic had nothing on this – we were actually strolling past lions, hyenas and rhino all just watching us and they were certainly not threatened by our presence on their patch. It was an exhilarating walk and much to our surprise when we got to the crest of the hill we were walking up, there before us out in the open was a breakfast table set up for us to take a break and feast with a view of wilderness and roaming animals for as far as the eye could see. Stunning.

Lane Baringo was next on the agenda. Lake Baringo is, after Lake Turkana, the most northern of the Kenyan Rift Valley lakes, with a surface area of 130 square kilometres (50 sq mi) and an elevation of 970 metres (3,180ft). The lake is fed by several rivers: the Molo, Perkerra and Ol Arabel. It has no obvious outlet; the waters are assumed to seep through lake sediments into the faulted volcanic bedrock. It is one of the two freshwater lakes in the Rift Valley in Kenya, the other being Lake Naivasha. The lake is in a remote hot and dusty area with over 470 species of birds, occasionally including migrating flamingos. A Goliath heronry is located on a rocky islet in the lake known as Gibraltar. The lake is part of the East African Rift system. The Tugen Hills, an uplifted fault block of volcanic and metamorphic rocks, lies west of the lake. The Laikipia Escarpment lies to the east. Water flows into the lake from the Mau Hills and Tugen Hills. It is a critical habitat and refuge for more than 500 species of birds and fauna, some of the migratory waterbird species being significant regionally and globally. The lake also provides a habitat for seven freshwater fish species. One being a Nile tilapia subspecies, this is endemic to the lake. Lake fishing is important to local social and economic development. The little canoe type boats that the locals fish in look much like a giant bunch of bananas. It is a wonder how they fish in these one-man canoes. A pleasure to watch. Additionally, the area is a habitat for many species of animals including the hippopotamus, Nile crocodile, and many other mammals, amphibians, reptiles and the invertebrate communities. While stocks of Nile tilapia in the lake are now low, the decline of this species has been mirrored by the success of another, the marbled lungfish which was introduced to the lake in 1974, and which now provides the majority of fish from the lake. Water levels have been reduced by droughts and over-irrigation. The lake is commonly turbid with sediment, partly due to intense soil erosion in the catchment area, especially on the Loboi Plain south of the lake.

A Kenyan Government report in 2021 estimated that the surface area of Lake Baringo had increased by over 100% to 268 square kilometres over the period 2010–2020. Lakeside villages were flooded and people displaced. There have also been increases in animal populations such as crocodiles, along with interactions between these animals and people. Unfortunately, when we visited, the local villages were suffering badly from drought and doing the rain dance every day for rain as crops were scarce and animals weak and thin. We stayed on Samatian Island, Ross and Caroline Withey's private island camp, where Caroline, Charlie and Dan grew up and called home for over 12 years, set on a private island on Lake Baringo in Kenya's Great Rift Valley. With its breathtaking views across the waters of the lake to the imposing backdrop of the Laikipia Escarpment, the island is perfect. The beauty of Baringo is legendary, with its spectacular sunsets, dazzling array of bird life, and the Njemps fishermen continuing a traditional lifestyle. Lake Baringo is also a Ramsar site, having been recognised internationally as a vitally important wetland. Samatian Island is the ultimate in relaxation in magical surroundings, which was perfect for our halfway through the trip holiday. On this island we enjoyed a few days of indulgence with bloody Marys in the infinity pool and full body massages together with specially guided bird viewing, picnics, bush breakfasts, cultural visits and a truly fabulous host. Me being the only single male on the trip had the luxury of an open room view under the stars with some of the most spectacular sunsets I've seen.

After a few days' rest and recuperation, we set off to our final destination: the Maasai Mara.

Maasai Mara, also sometimes spelt Masai Mara and locally known simply as The Mara, is a large national game reserve in Narok, Kenya, contiguous with the Serengeti National Park in Tanzania. It is named in honour of the Maasai people, the ancestral inhabitants of the area, who migrated to the area from the Nile Basin. Their description of the area when looked at from afar: "Mara" means "spotted" in the local Maasai language, because of the short bushy trees which dot the landscape. Maasai Mara is one of the wildlife conservation and wilderness areas in Africa, with its populations of lions, leopards, cheetahs and African bush elephants. It also hosts the Great Migration, which secured it as one of the Seven Natural Wonders of Africa, and as one of the ten Wonders of the World.

The Great Migration normally happens from July depending on weather as the wildebeest moves in large numbers crossing the river Mara from Tanzania. The Greater Mara ecosystem encompasses areas known as the Maasai Mara National Reserve, the Mara Triangle, several Maasai group ranches, and Maasai Mara conservancies. Blue wildebeest are the dominant inhabitants of the Maasai Mara. Around July of each year, these animals migrate north from the Serengeti plains in search of fresh pasture and return to the south around October. The Great Migration is one of the most impressive natural events worldwide. It involves some 1,300,000 blue wildebeest, 500,000 Thomson's gazelles, 97,000 topi, 18,000 common elands, and 200,000 Grant's zebras.

All members of the "Big Five" lions, African leopards, African bush elephants, African buffaloes and black rhinoceros are found all year round.

The Maasai Mara is the only protected area in Kenya with an indigenous black rhino population unaffected by translocations. Due to its size, the Mara can support one of the largest populations in Africa. The population of black rhinos was fairly numerous until 1960, but it was severely depleted by poaching in the 1970s and early 1980s, dropping to a low of 15 individuals. Numbers have been slowly increasing, but the population was still only up to an estimated 23 in 1999. The Mara Conservancy, one of the managing bodies of the reserve, reported 120 black rhinos in 1971 and 18 in 1984. They claimed one black rhino in 2001 when they began management and a stable 25-30 in 2023.

Hippopotamuses and Nile crocodiles are found in large groups in the Mara and Talek rivers. The plains between the Mara River and the Esoit Siria Escarpment are probably the best area for game viewing, in particular regarding lion and cheetah.

Large carnivores are found in the reserve. Lions are the most dominant and are found here in large numbers. Spotted hyenas are another abundant carnivore and will often compete with lions for food. Leopards are found anywhere in the reserve where there are trees for them to escape to. East African cheetahs are also found in high numbers on the open savanna, hunting gazelle and wildebeest. African wild dogs are quite rare here due to the widespread transmission of diseases like canine distemper and the heavy competition they face with lions, who can often ravage their populations. Their packs also roam and travel far distances throughout the plains, making it hard to track them. Smaller carnivores that don't directly compete with the latter include African wolves, black-backed jackals, African striped weasels, caracals, servals, honey badgers, aardwolves, African wildcats, side-striped jackals, bat-eared foxes, Striped polecats, African civets, genets, several mongoose species, and African clawless otters.

Antelopes can be found, including Grant's gazelles, impalas, duiker and Coke's hartebeests. The plains are also home to the distinctive Masai giraffe. The large roan antelope and the nocturnal bat-eared fox, rarely present elsewhere in Kenya, can be seen within the reserve borders.

The area has been named an Important Bird Area by BirdLife International. More than 500 species of birds have been identified in the park, many of which are migrants, with almost 60 species being raptors. It is an important area for the threatened birds that call this area home for at least part of the year. These include vultures, marabou storks, secretary birds, hornbills, crowned cranes, ostriches, long-crested eagles, African pygmy-falcons and the lilac-breasted roller, which is the national bird of Kenya. The resident Martial eagle is endangered. All of this was seen and photographed by our group. It was without doubt a once in a lifetime experience. Our stay was in Richard's Camp hosted by Edwina and Jay. All I can say about my special safari experience is, you can describe and try to explain the beauty of Kenya's wilderness, but nothing will ever beat the photographs of this amazing experience.

Figure 66 Hats for the Safari

Figure 67 Hat on and ready to go

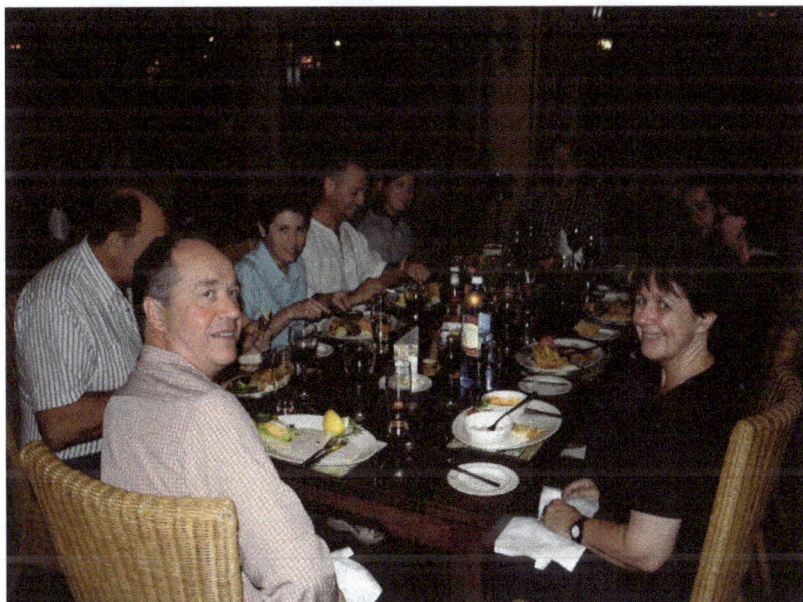

Figure 68 Arrival meal first day

Figure 69 Young Elephant

Figure 70 Young Rhino

Figure 71 Zebra

Figure 72Close up Elephant

Figure 73 Amazing so close to the wild

Figure 74 Our accommodation

Figure 75 Inside accommodation

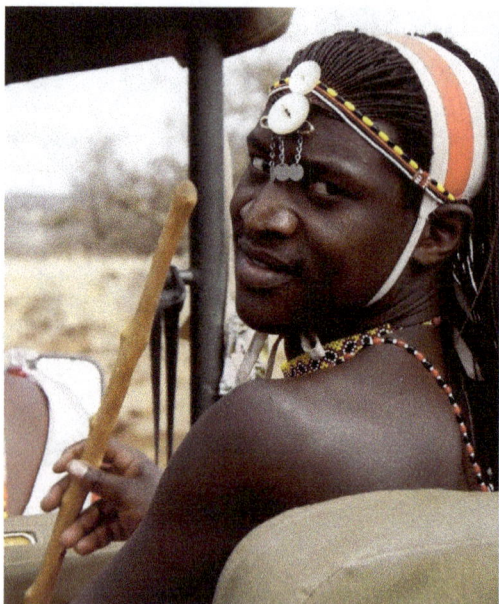

Figure 76 Maasai warrior guide

Figure 77 Maasai Warrior Guide

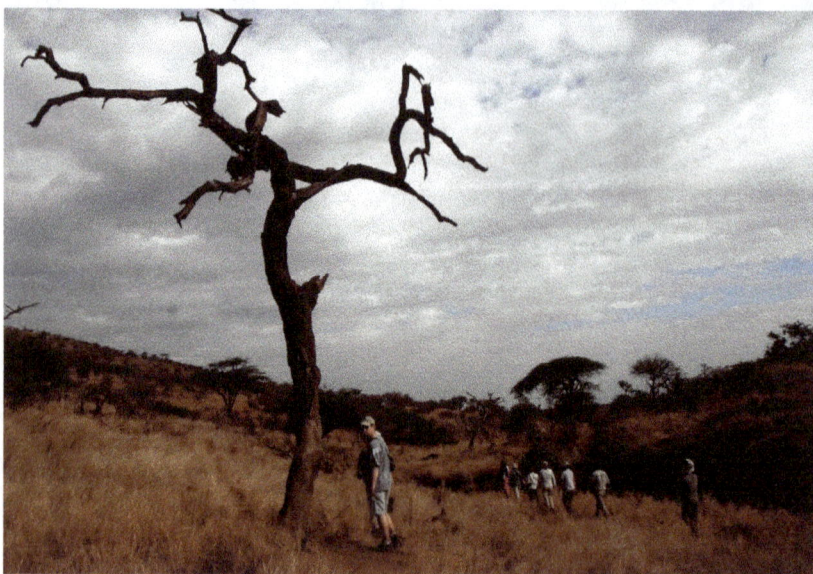

Figure 78 Out in the wild with armed guards

Figure 79 Wild Beauty

Figure 80 Ready, Chaps

Figure 81 On the move

Figure 82 Tribe Chief Figure 83 Chief's wife

Figure 84 Chief's accommodation

Figure 85 Wildebeest crossing

Figure 86 Feeding Time

Our three weeks flew by and before I knew it, I was back in Algeria, and on with the base extension.

My boss during this time was a Norwegian supply chain manager; however, his counterpart or his back-to-back was a very influential local Algerian who was an imam for the mosque. He was very much a do it as I say not as I do person. This caused us to fall out often. I recall having ordered a suppression system for the kitchen cooking area. This was a requirement of health and safety, but the system I ordered cost over $10,000. This was subsequently cancelled by the Algerian back-to-back as he deemed it too expensive. He was not a lover of the non-Muslim faiths anyway and did not like the fact that I would object to his reasoning. I recall him writing to BP's technical authority explaining that there was no need for fire suppression in the commercial kitchen. Obviously, he was told under no uncertain terms that a suppression system would be fitted. This did not do our relationship any favours. There was another time when the kitchen was being built with all the expensive equipment inside, it was a fenced off area as it was still a construction site, and you should only be in there with the correct PPE. I happened to be walking past when I noticed he was in with a crowd of his friends showing them around, all of them dressed in flip-flops and no PPE at all. It was my responsibility to keep order within the project construction, so I unfortunately had to remind him that he was not allowed inside the fenced area without the correct PPE. Again, this was another mark against me and he saw it as a personal vendetta. Unfortunately for me, at the end of the base extension, he managed to have me moved on. BP staff wanted to keep me because I've been involved from the start, and I handled the base well and was well liked by all. There was always a drive to localise all the positions, and he used that quite cleverly to get me moved on.

My boss, however, from Statoil secured a position for me in a new project, still for the same joint venture but in a place called In

Amenas. There was a new project starting called the compression project. In Amenas was home to one of the largest gas processing plants in Algeria. When you drill for gas, the gas is forced out of the ground under pressure; however, once the pressure in the cavity becomes equal to the pressure outside, the gas is no longer forced out of the cavity. The compression project was to build two large compressors that would reduce the pressure at the surface so as to suck more gas out of the cavity. This required us to first build a 400-man camp. This camp was to house the workers to build the compression project; consequently, I was moved to that area to set up and get prepared for the new camp build. Once again, I was involved in the build and design of the new base. This time the contract was won by a Japanese company called JCC. The engineering headquarters, however, was in the Philippines in Manila. My trip to Manila was far more exciting than my Turkey venture and once again more like a holiday than work.

It was during this time that some friends brought to my attention a property which was about to come on the market which had two acres of land with it. It had previously been part of a joint sale with the plot next door and Wimpey the house building company had provisional planning permission for 32 houses. The deal fell through because an argument developed between the neighbours for who was to receive the lion's share of the purchase; consequently, Wimpey moved on and purchased elsewhere. The house had been derelict for four years. The owner had moved into a bungalow due to his wife's failing mobility and she had then passed away. As a result, he just wanted a quick sale. It was a good buy, so I managed to agree a deal to avoid it being put on the market. I then had my architect view the land and come up with a new build project. He designed three spectacular properties at the time worth around £1.4 million each. Obviously having already purchased the existing property, I wanted to start work as soon as possible and not have it sat there whilst I was paying a mortgage. With this in mind my architect suggested we put planning in for the renovation of the existing property and then we could take our time with the close design of the other two. It was during this time on one of my rotational trips to Algeria that I discussed it with a close friend of mine, Carl. Carl was an American man who was married to a Dutch lady. He was a drilling engineer, and we had become very close friends. When he heard about my project he wanted to know if he could invest with me in the project. We discussed the details of the project in depth and decided to do it as a joint venture between the two of us. The first property took us just over a year to complete and we made the decision that I would sell my current house and move into the one we had just built there by releasing some of my mortgage to use as build capital for the other two properties. Plus, it meant I was living on site and could have a better handle on the workforce. Unfortunately, as luck would have it, we had a downturn in the building trade and a huge hike in material costs, in particular, wood. We made a start on the development of the other two properties in order to keep our planning. The rule was once you had planning permission you had to make a start within three years, failing this you would have to reapply for planning so in order to keep our planning, we made a substantial start – this way there was no rush to build the other two.

* * *

CHAPTER 14

❧

Algeria was becoming a little unstable. We had a small uprising
within our Algerian staff as the drivers were demanding more
money. There was a lot of local unrest and resistance to Western
workers having the majority of the oil and gas work. Local townships
wanted more of their population working within the oil and gas fields.
I recall one time during this unrest our bus from the base camp to
the airport was attacked with a small population throwing stones
and sticks, etc at the bus as we passed through their small village.
We have always had security in Algeria since my first visit. However,
it was always our own security, but because this was a joint venture
there was a big push to have local security supplied by Algeria with
only a couple of expats to run it. This drive was starting to take effect,
and we were constantly reduced in expat security. There is something
about having your own kind for security. It never made sense to me
having Islamic security to guard against Islamic fundamentalists.
There are too many holes in the structure to guarantee reliability. So,
we were basically left with a handful of Algerian gendarmerie and
our own local security guards with only two expat security. The only
ones permitted arms were the Algerian gendarmerie. The gendarmerie
has been severely tested in dealing with civil disorder since 1988. It
frequently has lacked sufficient manpower at the scene of disorder
and its units have been inadequately trained and equipped. As far
as our security goes they are not the best sole protection. I had just

returned to In Amenas after my Christmas break – we used to fly in from Gatwick Airport to Hassi Messaoud then get a small charter flight out to the field to In Ameanas airport then a bus ride to the base camp. Although this was a dry camp a blind eye was often turned when expats brought in the occasional bottle of wine or alcohol, together with some often-missed treats like bacon and sausages. We would usually have a small get together particularly on the last night before going on leave. I recall getting an invite over to the security boys' room for a farewell beverage and a bacon toastie. Because I was ex-military, I often got asked over by the security boys. I recall on this occasion Paul was going on leave in the morning looking forward to going on holiday with his girl. During our gathering I was informed there was going to be an exercise whereby they may want to utilise our project's ambulances. I agreed this would not be a problem and thought nothing more about it. We had an enjoyable night, and I wished Paul a good leave.

It was 05:20 when I was standing in my towel having a shave when I thought for a second, I heard gunfire. You know that feeling when you think to yourself did I hear that or not? Then my phone rang, when I answered it was my friend Peter, the construction engineer I worked with. I think there is gunfire outside, he said in a rather panic-stricken voice. Okay, I answered, just stay where you are, and I will get dressed and find out what's happening and get back to you. I know they are having an exercise so it might just be that. Emergency response exercises were often done to ensure everyone is conversant with the accident and emergency protocol should an incident ever happen, such as an explosion within the gas plant or a major fire. Before I had time to get dressed, he was back on the phone saying it's definitely gunfire. There are tracer rounds heading over towards the military camp. Tracer ammunition, or tracers, are bullets or cannon-calibre projectiles that are built with a small pyrotechnic charge in their base. When fired, the pyrotechnic composition is ignited by the burning powder and burns very brightly, making the projectile trajectory visible to the naked eye during daylight, and very bright during night time firing. This allows the shooter to visually trace the trajectory of the projectile and thus make necessary ballistic corrections, without having to confirm projectile impacts and without even using the sights of the weapon. Tracer fire can also be used as a marking tool to signal other shooters to concentrate their fire on a particular target during battle. Usually, every third round that comes out of the weapon is visible. This also confirms they are live rounds which means only one thing. We are under attack.

I finished getting dressed and looked outside the door of my cabin and sure enough we were under fire. My mind was now racing. This was totally alien to me to be in an attack with no weapons or anything to defend myself. I picked up my phone and called Paul, one of our security guys. There was no answer. Unbeknown to me at this time but Paul was already dead.

The bus with all the lads going home on leave had left the base already, when the attack began. Fortunately for them, transport to and from the base always had military escorts. The dull sound of fire I thought I'd heard was in fact at a good distance which is why I had questioned the sound. But that sound was the bus coming under attack as it met the terrorists heading towards the base. It wasn't till a break off group had reached the base that it became apparent we were being attacked. Failing to get hold of Paul, I then tried the other Security expat Yann who was a Frenchman ex French special forces but there was no answer from him either. By now there was a lot of commotion going on with a lot of people running around. My next call was to Fitz, Paul's back-to-back, I knew he was in Gatwick waiting to board the plane to relieve Paul from his post. He answered the phone, and I explained to him that we were under attack and what the current situation was. He replied saying they had already been informed, and the flight had been cancelled. He also said he had to put me through to the emergency response team. I was put through to the team and we talked in depth about what was happening and what the current situation was. I could see from my window that the terrorists were letting the local Algerians go and many of the Algerians were making their exit. What we didn't know was the size of the terrorist group nor what their objective was. This, however, was at a time when they were taking foreign hostages and cutting their heads off on TV. So, we had to naturally presume it was us they were looking for. During the attack, the terrorists accidentally shot out the generators supplying power to the base; consequently, we were plunged into darkness bar the emergency light system. Whilst talking to the emergency response team, I explained that we only had a matter of hours before communication would be non-existent. After all, we need power for the communication towers to work and being part of the maintenance and knowing the site I knew the back-up power would not last longer than three to four hours. Exactly four hours later, we lost all communication.

My cabin was opposite the kitchens and there were several containers at the other side of the road opposite my window. These containers stored all the kitchen food and supplies. My cabin overlooked the road and there was a streetlight right outside my window. I had previously covered my window with black paper to stop the light from shining in when I slept. I had torn a small corner off the paper so I could observe what was happening outside. There was still a lot of commotion. I recall a couple of Algerians coming out of their cabins and as they started down the road, they were shouted at by the terrorists Something in Arabic and they would put their hands up and go back into their cabins. I later found out what they were shouting. They were smashing the doors shouting, "We're only looking for foreigners, you Algerians can go!" It was clear I could not leave my cabin yet, especially if they were looking for expats. It was a frightening time as

I knew they were looking for us, yet I was unable to leave the cabin, particularly as it was still daylight, my mind still racing as to what to do. A few more hours went by and there was still a lot of gunfire going on between the terrorists and the military guard. I knew I would have to wait till dusk before leaving my cabin, otherwise I would surely be seen. Then I heard shouts in broken English saying you can come out now it's safe. My military training taught me to trust no one in situations like this, especially someone shouting it's safe in broken English. Our living accommodation was nothing more than the size of a small caravan. It consisted of a very small bathroom with a toilet and shower cubicle. And a very small room which contained a single bed, a sink, a small fridge and a small metal cupboard divided into two sections. One for myself and one for my back-to-back. The cupboard was so small it was impossible to squeeze more than four or five coat hangers in there.

Fortunately, I'm really fussy when it comes to hygiene and I had brought all my own bedding and pillows, etc. I did not want to use the same bedding that was issued and shared with my back-to-back. I knew now they were doing room searches looking for us but with nowhere to go what could I do in such a small room? So I quickly made my bed and folded the sheets back like the room boys did when they made the beds. We had a washing bag which was a net bag we would leave our clothes in to be laundered. I put this on the bottom of the bed and on the floor at the side of the bed I left a pair of boots side by side. I made my room look like it was empty. I then got all of the old bedding and climbed under the bed pulling the old bedding to cover me. I knew that the room searches would have to be quick as they had a lot of rooms to get through. Making the room up like it had just been made gave the impression that there was no one in the room and perhaps I was one of the people on the bus going on leave. It's not much but at the time it's all I could come up with and I just lay still, hoping it would work. Time seems to drag when you're waiting but sure enough it wasn't long before my door was kicked open. I heard someone come into the room but only for a few seconds then some shouting and more commotion and I heard the door swing back closed. I lay as still as I could be, hoping that my plan had worked. My heart was racing and all I had in my head was the thought of all those prisoners previously in orange suits getting their heads cut off on TV. It was a terrifying thought. I could hear the continuation of the rooms being checked as the noise was slowly getting further away from me. Eventually, I crawled out from under the bed.

Because it was just after Christmas on my return through Gatwick, I had purchased some small Santa Claus shaped shortbread biscuit tins, and I used them to give to the locals as little gifts. I had one tin left which housed about eight small round shortbreads. I also had one apple and six 1.5L bottles of water. I used to always bring Berocca with me, which is an effervescent vitamin tablet which I dissolved in the water bottles. I put three bottles in my backpack together with my apple and the shortbread, and prepared for my dusk escape.

By now the attack had hit the news headlines and people in the UK were waking up to the news of the attack. The Government summoned an immediate Cobra meeting to discuss what to do next. The problem for foreign countries is that Algeria does not want foreign help and prefers to deal with this type of incident in-house. In the meantime, it was starting to get dusk. I had been in this predicament for almost 12 hours now. It was time to look for a way out. I had told my friend Peter to wait in his room and if I found a way out, I would come and get him, but I had no idea if they had checked his accommodation yet or if he was even still alive. Our accommodation caravans were mounted on concrete blocks and raised slightly off the ground. This not only helped to level them, but it also went some way to keeping scorpions and other critters from climbing into the accommodation. The units were also positioned in long rows. I kept very low, slowly making my way towards the perimeter security fence. Pausing, lying on my stomach between each accommodation block. I did not want to make any noise or alert anyone who might be in the accommodation, particularly other Muslim locals as you can't trust anyone but yourself in these circumstances. I eventually got to the open road, and I lay on my stomach assessing the obstacles ahead of me. I had about four metres of open gravel then a five-metre-wide tarmac road to cover, another six or so metres of open ground then a five-metre-high fence with razor wire coiled on top. Another five-metre gap to another five-metre fence again with razor wire coiled on top. After that it was an open desert. I was debating how to get past my obstacles. I couldn't climb the fence as it would be too noisy and at great risk, especially trying to get through the razor wire only to face the same challenge five metres further on. I doubted I could dig under the fence because we were in the process of building a new extension to the base and the fence we had just constructed had a metre of concrete foundation throughout its length. This was to prevent wild dogs from burrowing into the base camp. The fence was a well-constructed security fence which was designed to keep intruders out; however, when you're in and need to get out it's not so user friendly. To add to my concern, if I did manage to get out what would I be running into, bearing in mind we have possibly got Algerian security forces on the other side who could easily mistake me for a terrorist? Not only that, but they were very well known for being trigger happy. It was at that time I looked to my right toward the communications tower. I saw two armed terrorists with a local Algerian; they were looking at the communications tower. I'm quite sure they were trying to get him to re-establish communications – after all, if we have now lost all communication signals, they would have too. It was becoming clear to me that I would not find my escape route here. I decided to make my way back to my accommodation and re-think. I thought it would be safer, especially as they had already done a clearance check on it. So, I made my way slowly and cautiously back. When I got back into my accommodation, I lay on my bed, my mind racing, not knowing what to do next. I lay on my mattress because it was more comfortable. It was January and the winter nights in the desert are extremely cold. Fortunately, when we built the base camp, we covered the area in gravel. This was to avoid the sand being blown into the accommodation blocks but the advantage for me was I could hear footsteps on the gravel if they came near my accommodation. Each time I heard footsteps; I would get back under the bed. During the night, I could hear occasional gunfire and helicopter gunships circling above. The worrying thought for me was why is it taking so long to rescue us? How many terrorists are there? Each passing day became more worrying; not only that but I would soon run out of food and water so I would have no choice but to try and escape. I used to pee in the sink to avoid going to the bathroom because the bathroom floor was extremely squeaky. In reality it probably couldn't be heard from outside but when you're in hiding every little noise is amplified in your mind. The frustrating part for me was every night a couple of terrorists would drive our vehicles and park right outside my accommodation and get food from the containers opposite me. I could literally watch them from my window. They were only about five or six metres away. I recall one night hearing footsteps on the gravel close to my accommodation. I got back under the bed and stayed there. I was there for a good few hours when suddenly I felt wet. I climbed out only to find that the water had come from the fridge freezer defrosting and I now had a large puddle of water on the floor to contend with.

I remained in my room, unable to get out for three long days and on the fourth day I decided I had to leave as I had no more shortbread and only my apple and water left. I crouched down and looked out of my window to see if I could see any activity. Suddenly an armed man appeared from the side of one of the food containers. I didn't recognise the uniform so presumed it was another terrorist. I quickly got back under the bed. Then I heard a knocking on the door and once again in broken English was you can come out now it's safe. After a few more attempts, I heard the footsteps on the gravel moving away. My heart was pounding, and I thought to myself I wonder if they have found the tee cards we use between bases.

We used to have a tee card system for entering and leaving the base. This was a card which was shaped like a T. In the Guard house you would have an in and out section. If you left the base to go down to the central processing facility. You would take out your tee card and put it in the out tray. The accommodation base was some 3km away from the processing plant. This was due to the blast area. Should the processing facility blow up, the accommodation base had to be outside the blast zone. So, the tee cards were to let key personnel know who was on the base and who was at the processing plant in case of an emergency or fire. The worrying part was if the terrorists were smart enough, they would have got the tee cards which had a picture of ourselves on the card together with our room number.

Unbeknown to me at this time, fortunately when the attack took place, the Algerian guard was smart enough to get rid of the tee cards. Sadly, he was unfortunately shot during the attack. I do believe his actions probably saved us from being found a lot quicker. About five or ten minutes went by then I heard more footsteps coming towards my accommodation. This time I could tell there were several people, not just one. Again, I had banging on my door and banging on my windows calling, you can come out now, it's safe. I was now starting to panic. Have they found the tee cards? Have they finally caught me? Again, the footsteps went away only to return five minutes later; however, this time I heard a key go into my door. My heart stopped. They'd found the keys and know I'm here. I heard the door open then I heard a voice say, Allen, it's me, Jamal. I recognised the voice of one of my Algerian colleagues. I pulled the covers from over my head and peered out from under the bed. I recognised two Algerian soldiers by their uniform. They had their weapons trained on me as they did not know if I was armed or not. Algerian military, I said, and they moved their guns away. I came out from under the bed, and they gave me a bottle of water and a Mars bar. They took me to a safe holding area where my friend Peter was stood. He smiled at me and came and gave me a big hug. The reason they came to your room three times he said was because each time they told me you were not there, and I told them he will definitely be there but he won't come out unless you drag him out. We both laughed. He had been fortunate that nobody had even come to his room. We were the last three to be rescued, but before leaving, we had to make a statement with the Algerian authorities who then took us to the airport. The company that used to look after us with regards to flights was a company called Jet Air. Fortunately for us, they managed to hire Alan Sugar's private jet to come and collect us.

The air hostesses were trying to be very nice to us and they had some bottles of champagne to celebrate our release. Although it was nice of them none of us were in the mood for celebrations as we had just lost 40 good colleagues. We landed at Gatwick Airport in a special area whereby we were taken inside to a holding area where we had to give a debrief, forensics took samples from us, and we had to sit down and write a detailed statement. After a couple of hours, we were finally allowed to leave. My partner at the time had been told that I was killed, and it wasn't until I managed to get a satellite phone while still in the field to call her and let her know I was okay. She met me at Gatwick and after the debrief we spent the night at the Hilton in Gatwick before driving home to Plymouth.

When I arrived home, I was inundated with press and media trying to get a story out of me. The Devon and Cornwall police were amazing, and they had a car outside keeping the press away which was a great help as I just wanted a bit of normalisation.

I had been home for two days when I received a call from a special investigation unit who were looking into the incident and because I was the last one out and I had lots of photos of the bodies that were scattered around and video footage of quite a lot of the area, they wanted to come and see me. They arrived a couple of days later and we spent two days doing an in-depth timeline of the incident. There were 40 deaths excluding the terrorists and although a lot had been killed by the terrorists there were also a lot killed by the Algerian forces too. After all, the gas plant was about 10% of Algeria's income, bringing in around ten and a half million dollars a day out of the ground. So, it's understandable that the military directive was at no cost do these terrorists reach the processing plant. The terrorists used expats as shields as they drove towards the gas plant, but the helicopter gunships did not worry about the captives; they were only interested in stopping the terrorists reaching the plant. Unlike the rest of the countries affected, they viewed it differently. At the crisis room at BP's international headquarters in St James's Square, London, decisions were prioritised by the order "PEP": "people, environment and property".

Almost the complete opposite to the Algerian process.

There were many parts to the attack which when you're in the middle of it you don't see.

For example, the terrorists were very well informed. They had detailed maps and timings from inside information given to them. They were late at getting to the site due to a vehicle accident on the way to the base. Unfortunately for them but fortunately for us, the petroleum engineer who knew the gas plant was killed en route. This is what delayed their arrival. They were supposed to arrive before the bus carrying all the expats going home on crew change left the base. The bus had already left the base under military escort. This was not part of the plan and why the bus was attacked some distance from the base. This is also when the terrorists group split up. Several were in a fire fight with the military escort whilst others sped towards the accommodation base. The military escort managed to protect the bus and get the passengers off and into safety. The remaining terrorists then joined their colleagues heading for the accommodation with the intent to capture expats. The Algerian guard, hearing the attack, immediately got rid of the tee cards which had the names and room numbers of everyone on the base. As the terrorists smashed through the entrance the Algerian guard was shot dead. Little did he know just how important that decision was to all of us in hiding. Panic was now spreading throughout the base. From 6am for several hours, the gunmen began a frenzied hunt for foreigners. One Algerian worker said: "They told us: 'We have nothing against you Algerians, you can take your things and leave.' They said they wanted expats and that they would find them." There were several volleys of Kalashnikov fire and rounds of grenade explosions, then militants went from door to door of the foreigners' living quarters, shooting out locks and searching bedrooms, dragging workers from under beds and behind cupboards. Several Filipino workers who refused to leave their rooms were beaten. Foreigners were rounded up, many had their hands tied behind their backs with rubber cable-ties, others had their mouths taped. The terrorists, which Algerian officials said included at least three explosives' experts, set about strapping Semtex bombs around the necks and waists of some of the hostages. Some survivors said foreigners were shot as they ran to escape, and numerous foreigners were killed with a bullet to the head. When militants saw that there were mainly Japanese, Filipino or Malaysians in the block, a commander was heard to say he wanted Americans, French and English and "didn't need Asians". Obviously, these were considered more valuable as a ransom tool.

The terrorists were now starting to prepare a splinter group to get into the central processing plant. Their intention was to blow it up – after all, they see it as a symbol of western capitalism. In the meantime, an SAS unit was sent to Cyprus in preparation, two high-ranking SAS officers, accompanied by MI6 operatives, flew to Algeria on the Thursday night. They based themselves at the British Embassy in Algiers and sent valuable information back to London. The big problem was, however, Algeria will not allow foreign help. There was such a disconnect between Whitehall and Algiers over how to handle the hostage crisis. Our government was bewildered by the Algerian decision to open fire without consulting us or other foreign leaders. But the Algerian army had – and still has – three simple reasons for cracking down at once: it wanted to stifle the crisis quickly and to destroy the terrorists; they wanted to show their own people that the regime is still firmly in charge, and they were also desperate to avoid any chance of Western special forces getting to play a role on their territory. The signal to any terrorists who enter Algeria was that they will not survive, and the Algerian people will not be intimidated or held to ransom.

The terror chief behind the attack was Mokhtar Belmokhtar, a 40-year-old one-eyed Algerian, dubbed the Marlboro Man because he funds terrorist activities by smuggling cigarettes. A video was aired of him saying: We in Al Qaeda announce this blessed operation, we are ready to negotiate with the West and the Algerian government provided they stop their bombing of Mali's Muslims. This obviously fell on deaf ears. After all, nobody negotiates with terrorism.

The four-day siege reached its climax after seven workers were executed in a final, monstrous act of violence by their Al Qaeda-linked captors just as special forces soldiers stormed the desert gas facility to try to rescue them, they were tied to the huge gas pipes and blown up. The bloody end to the Saharan siege exposed the full scale of the diplomatic rift between the British and Algerian governments during the crisis.

The confusion continued when the Algerians publicly declared the operation to be over while the British diplomats were still maintaining that it was ongoing and dangerous. The Foreign Office later explained that it was reluctant to declare the siege at an end while a number of Britons remained unaccounted for. It was a day later when I was finally rescued, and as I walked away from the carnage, forensic experts were trying to piece together the charred remains of the guys who were blown up.

After any incident like this there is always questions as to how and why this could be allowed to happen. Below is an extract of the case study for this attack.

IN AMENAS CASE STUDY

On 16th January 2013, a terrorist attack occurred at the In Amenas gas plant. This plant was a joint venture with European (Statoil and BP) and Algerian (Sonatrach) interests. The attack concluded on 19th January with the loss of 40 on site employees, and the death of 29 terrorists. The mastermind behind this attack was an Algerian terrorist, Mokhtar Belmokhtar, with close links to al-Qa'ida (Combating Terrorism Centre, 2023).

The backdrop to this event was political instability in the surrounding regions. From 2011 the regional security situation deteriorated. The civil war and chaos in Libya had a destabilising impact on the wider area. Close by, Northern Mali was known as an area that would offer sanctuary to terrorist groups. The concerns regarding the regional security situation were known to the joint venture group. It seems that investigations into the attack have also revealed concerns that the terrorists 'benefited from insider knowledge in their planning of the attack'. This was supported by both the Algerian officials and Statoil investigators (Combating Terrorism Centre, 2013).

The exact motive for the attack at In Amenas remains uncertain, however a strong possibility is that it was to take hostages for ransom and increase the coffers of the terrorist group. Aligned to this is competition that existed between various Islamic groups to 'outbid' each other and this may have been part of it. It had been suggested that the attack may have been a response to French air strikes in Northern Mali, but it appears that the planning for this attack began months before the air strikes (Combating Terrorism Centre, 2015).

The sum of outer and inner security measures failed to protect people at the site from the attack on In Amenas on 16th January. The Algerian military were not able to detect and prevent the attackers from reaching the site. Security measures at the site were not constructed to withstand or delay an attack of this scale and relied on military protection working effectively. Physical protective measures were constructed on the assumption that the Algerian military would prevent and protect against an armed assault. This assumption also underpinned their security plans and security risk management (Statoil, 2013). It is evident that there was an over reliance on Algerian military to provide the level of protection needed at the site, however given the size of the area involved there was always the possibility that an attack would get through that first line of defence. Security protection closer to the site was too frail for such an important multinational operation. An investigation commissioned by Statoil made a number of recommendations, including (1) Security at In Amenas: Improve the joint ventures ability to detect, delay and stop potential attacks by reinforcing electronic and physical protective measures, enhancing its security risk management capability and develop a coherent programme of security training and exercising. (2) Organisation and Capabilities: Develop a clearly defined ambition for the Company's security capability. Strengthen the total security organization. Ensure an holistic approach to security. (3) Risk Management Systems: develop a security risk management system that is dynamic, fit for purpose and geared towards action (Statoil, 2013).

This investigation and review concluded that there was no evidence discovered indicating that anyone within the joint venture had advance warning of this specific attack, although the report did highlight the need for such ventures to be more aware of the strategic threats that exist and to take actions commensurate with these threats (Statoil, 2013). Whilst it appears that there was no specific intelligence about this attack, the environment at the time should not have made this type of attack unthinkable (Combating Terrorism Centre, 2023).

The potential for such attacks should have been planned for. In fact, as part of the review Statoil (2013) suggested that 'Companies should consider and think through the implications of scenarios where security layers break down'. This level of preparation and planning ties in with FEMA (2012) who advised that 'While not intended to be predictive of what the future holds, scenario planning offers a robust structure for thinking about alternative – and plausible – future operating environments.'

During the UK Inquest into the deaths of the seven Britons who died at the site, the judge was critical of the plant's management and their failures to upgrade protection. The judge highlighted the rarity of security drills, no armed guards protecting the living areas and the true nature of dangers in the area were obscured within the risk assessments (The Guardian, 2015).

It is noteworthy that this investigation and the subsequent report were commissioned by Statoil and that one of the key findings within it is that Statoil's contribution to the overall emergency response was effective and professional and suggested that the Statoil leadership had set clear parameters that the whole organization had mobilized around. And yet despite this, within the actual recommendations of the review, under the heading of Emergency Preparedness and Response the recommendation was to 'Coordinate and standardize emergency response planning consistent with the principles of the Incident Command System (ICS)' (Statoil 2013). It seems that question marks remained about the overall response approach. When it comes to the ICS, the caution from Rubens, 2023 should be heard, 'And yet, when it comes to actual incident management, the ICS itself is often the first point of failure'. The operational crisis management system must be simple, everything else can be complex (Rubens, 2023).

Within the review the positive feedback from survivors and next of kin on follow up and support provided by Statoil is referenced. The review team believed that the approach and resources made available after the incident to support those involved should be included as part of the Company's future processes (Statoil, 2013). Whilst this is positive, it does appear that the immediate emergency response on the ground was uncoordinated and there was no state of preparedness for such an attack. In fact, as the UK Inquest determined that Algerian gendarmes arrived long after the main compound had been seized by terrorists and security training drills were a rarity (Guardian, 2015).

Hindsight tends to make what was once improbable now seem inevitable and to turn weak signals into strong warnings (Statoil, 2013). However, it is worth noting here a warning from Rubens, 2023, that security failures happen when security teams do not think something will happen today. This security failure seems to have been a lack of preparedness for the possibility of such an attack taking place and not being responsive to geopolitical issues that had the real potential to impact the site.

The shortcomings within security protection at In Amenas reveal a regime that was not alive to the issues unfolding in the wider yet connected regions. This does not appear to have been properly considered as part of the risk management process and consequently did not influence the introduction of a more effective security regime at the site. As proffered by Rubens, 2023, 'The main reason for a failure in security is because security management was weak.'.

A number of the lessons that emerged from the In Amenas tragedy can translate into good practice recommendations. These include.

1. 'Security in Depth' principles should be applied. The importance of applying greater levels of security in depth cannot be overstated as Martin, 2019 contributes, 'Each layer of protective security potentially provides opportunities to detect that an attack is underway, delay the attackers and mount a response before the attackers have time to do more harm'. The over reliance on Algerian military to protect the plant from terrorist attack meant that insufficient use of other layered security created a huge risk which was exploited by the terrorists. This would be a vulnerability anywhere in the world and failure to put such layered measures in place exposes entities to higher levels of threat from terrorists globally.

2. Exercise/Learn/test and validate. The Statoil review did not reference a planned for or implemented evacuation process during this attack, meaning that those at the site had limited guidance on what to do in the event of an attack such as this.

They were largely left to their own devices until military/ Government/Company responses were put in place. The critical need to exercise and test procedures for effectiveness should be obvious. If these procedures are not run through to improve everyone's state of readiness, then the overall response will ultimately be substandard. Improve capability development by going live and continue to practise, this should help to create resilience (Rubens, 2023). As part of this test and integrate the JESIP principles into the overall response (JESIP, 2023).

3. Conduct an effective, site and locality specific risk assessment, which is a living document. There were concerns raised around the scope of the risk assessment for In Amenas. It failed to capture and consider the significance of regional geopolitical events and the potential impact from these on In Amenas (Statoil, 2013). Environmental scanning and being security sensitive to what is happening at the edges of your area of responsibility should become part of the risk assessment process. This should not be a static document but should be living and updated as and when relevant matters arise and should have regular management and corporate level oversight to ensure that any remedial action needed is progressed at the earliest opportunity.

In conclusion, the In Amenas attack should have been better prepared for and despite the review identifying positives within the post event response, there were shortcomings in the levels of protection and overall preparedness at the plant to deter or delay a terrorist attack. There is learning from these events that was outlined within the Statoil review recommendations, but unfortunately despite the passage of time, it is possible that they could still be applied to the next local/ National/Global crisis management response. A fair question for some may be, 'how much learning has there been from previous events?'.

Figure 87 In Amenas Arial View

Figure 88 GasPlant

Figure 89 Office Block

Figure 90 Captured Weapons

Figure 91 Carnage after Helicopter gunship attack

Figure 92 Fallen Terrorists

Figure 93 Military securing area

* * *

CHAPTER 15

After the attack I was off work for almost a year on full pay as the damage to the plant was repaired and security provisions recommended after the case study were put in place. I was asked if I would be happy to return to complete the project we had started. The day rate of course was raised to a sensible level considering the risk and I agreed to return. I stayed for a further three years from 2014 to 2017 before we finally completed the project and handed it over. My time in Algeria had sadly come to an end having started as just an off chance, one off contract for only three weeks in 1996 to finally leaving in 2017 – a good 21 years. I still can't believe it. The million-dollar question was what should I do now.

Having been on a three weeks on, three weeks off rotation whilst in the oil and gas industry I was fortunate enough to have travelled to most countries in the world. There are not many places I have not been to. My favourite country I have visited is Vietnam. Vietnam has endured foreign intrusions by various countries, Portugal, the Netherlands, France, China, Japan, Soviet Union, Laos, Cambodia, South Korea and the United States. For some three-quarters of a century, until after World War II, Vietnam was a French colony. But eventually every invader was driven off. Their people are so nice and as a nation they are so resilient you just have to respect that. Another country I like is the Netherlands, particularly Amsterdam;

it is a wonderful diverse country, they are well renowned for their liberal lifestyles. It was in fact my experiences in the Netherlands that lay the foundation for my next adventure.

The housing market and construction industry was still in a downturn and had not recovered. I was finding it very difficult to get a sale on the house. It was valued at £1.4 million, but you don't get £1.4 million buyers in Plymouth. I was now out of work and no longer in the oil and gas industry. The construction industry was at a standstill so I was unable to get the finance needed to continue building, so I had to look at some way of earning money at the same time as trying to save our investment. It's so difficult when you're in a spot to come up with inventive ideas to survive. It was during this time that I remembered one of my visits to the Netherlands. I had been invited to a rather posh dinner event. The event was actually held in a restaurant within a windmill. I recall meeting all the people that arrived, and it just so happened that the lady and man sat opposite me were the only ones to arrive in their own helicopter. We got chatting and although I don't like asking people what they do for a living I was burning with curiosity as they were obviously very well to do. In the end, I did ask him and he replied that he runs a club. A club? I asked, you've made all your money from running a club? No, he replied. I used to be a farmer and I have quite a few outbuildings on my land and I decided to turn them into a club. This is my sole income now and I have given up farming. How long are you in Holland? He asked me. I'm here for another two weeks, I replied. Okay, why don't I send my driver to pick you up at the weekend and you can come and have a look at my club and be my guest? That's very kind of you, I replied, I would love to. I didn't think any more of it until the following Saturday when I was being picked up. His club was halfway between Amsterdam and Rotterdam in the middle of nowhere. It took us just over an hour to get there with his driver. We arrived before opening time which gave us time to have a look around the grounds. The location was stunning, and the property looked like an old Hansel and Gretel movie. Upon entering the grounds you went through a large, impressive gate with two Cupids firing an arrow into a heart. The heart being the gate. It soon became apparent that this club wasn't what I would call a nightclub which I had envisaged; it was in fact a high-end swingers club, the likes I've never come across. I had no idea, although that said I should've guessed by the title of the club known as Fun4two. The decor was immaculate and high-end, you had a large dance floor, a large bar area, a restaurant overlooking the dance floor and upstairs you had a large Jacuzzi and swimming pool with sauna, steam rooms and Tantric rooms. The whole place was like a maze with various playrooms and theme rooms all over the place. You could literally get lost just walking around. After my introductory walk around, I sat at the bar talking with the owners as the place started to fill up. It was an interesting concept to come into the club. You have to become a member as it was a members-only club, prior to becoming a member you would be vetted by the owners. Once a member you paid €130 entrance fee that entitled you to everything. Free food, free drinks and free locker room for changing outfits. The couples coming in were extremely elegant and smartly dressed as there was a dress code to enter. Most of the ladies were sitting around the bar drinking champagne. Everyone was extremely friendly and very easy to get on with. The guests were from all over the world. The gates to the club opened at 8 o'clock and closed at 10 o'clock. There was no more entrance after 10 so if you were coming, you had to be punctual or you would not gain entry. The night I was there there was a total of some 350 guests. When you consider the club is open Thursday to Sunday that's quite a good earner. Another interesting concept to do with his club was that at 11:30 a signature tune would be played by the DJ which indicated that everyone had to strip down to their underwear. This was an extremely good idea considering the type of club it was and it seemed to have the desired effect and put everyone in the same environment. People seemed to just relax and enjoy themselves. They were still dancing away on the dance floor, sitting at the bar, eating in the restaurant and just casually wandering around enjoying the arena when and where they wanted. It was certainly an eye-opener for me. I ended up leaving with lots of friends to keep in touch with, having had an excellent evening. The lifestyle was not one I would choose but wow what a great business concept.

So here I was, out of work, unable to continue the building project due to the current climate, wondering how I could earn a good living. I wondered if such a club concept would work in the UK. I know the British are quite prudish when compared with the Dutch, but things in the UK seemed to be opening up. I mean, let's face it, in my days there were two sexes, male and female. Now I'm totally lost. So, I decided to look into the swinging scene in the UK. Obviously opening such a club, I needed to look at the legal side as well as doing some research. My findings were astonishing. I visited two separate solicitors – one happened to be female, the other male; both of the solicitors were well averse to the scene. Surely that can't be a coincidence. It turned out during my research that there are actually 11 million plus swingers in the UK, that basically equates to one in six. I guess when you sit down and think about it, there is such a diverse climate in sexuality nowadays, can you remember when it was LGBT? Now it's LGBTIQCAPGNGFNBA stands for Lesbian, Gay, Bisexual, Transgender, Intersex, Questioning, Curious, Asexual, Pansexual, Gender Nonconforming, Gender-Fluid, Non-Binary and Androgynous. On top of that you have polyamorous relationships and gay marriages popping up all over the place. So, I guess the world is changing, so why not? Why can't I have such an exclusive club in the UK?

It was a difficult dilemma. I knew the club concept in the Netherlands works and works well, but I needed to get another opinion on whether I should try it in the UK. One of my very close friends whom I have always had a connection with would be the ideal person to discuss this with. Nyree is a stunning blonde lady who has the same sense of adventure as me. She says it as it is and is not afraid of anything – if she thought it would be a good idea then you can rest assured that it would work. I have known Nyree for many years, and we have always connected on every front so when it comes to opinions she is a good source to check. I wasn't at all surprised that Nyree thought the concept was a good idea, but wanted first hand experience first before committing. Of course I was always up for another investigative trip to the Netherlands. So we planned another visit, bringing along a few friends to help make that important decision. Needless to say, it was a big hit.

During my research I found there were a few clubs in the UK specifically for the swinging scene; however, these clubs were what I would call sticky carpet or dirty old men's clubs. They didn't seem to harness the classiness that people prefer. Nothing like Fun4two. I also found there were several websites set up specifically for the swinging scene such as Fab swingers or SDS. These both had an extremely large membership. I joined Fab swingers to investigate the membership numbers and how many potential clients I could have. To my astonishment if I typed in say a five mile radius from where I was in Plymouth, there would always be over 300 members actually online as I looked. That's a big market. Fab Swingers has a membership of over 300,000. They charge £5 per month. So just do the maths on that.

I had found my next venture. Could I get it off the ground?

During my research two friends of mine were instrumental in helping me along the way. They were husband and wife and very keen to help. I hosted three parties to test the waters to see if this adventure would actually work. Being totally new to the scene and somewhat a novice, the parties went a long way into teaching me the etiquette in this lifestyle. Our first party we had around ten couples turn up which was ok but nowhere near what was needed for a club, but then again, we were the new kids on the block. The party was a success, and everyone put good reviews on the Fab Swingers website. On our second party we more than doubled the couples who attended and once again had some great reviews. By the time we got to our third-party, we were turning people away because we couldn't fit any more into the house and it was a very large house. On the third-party we had over 65 couples. This was building up to be an exciting venture.

The first thing I needed was the right property, so I started looking at properties on the market. It took several months before I came across a property called Croydon Hall. This was a stunning property out of the way of the public eye and for me ticked all the boxes for a club and hotel. It was nestled in five acres of spectacular Somerset countryside, and just to set the scene you had to drive through a few miles of country roads before you came across this stunning property. There were very limited neighbours and the ones that were around were out of sight, so very private. I thought this was the perfect place. The problem was it was at the top end of my budget. I discussed the property with my two friends in great detail and they were also keen to join the adventure. So, we decided that if they came along with me, I would use all my capital to buy and renovate the property and they would sell their house and we would use the equity on their property to fund us till we got going. I arranged a viewing and went down to visit the site which only added to my determination, once I had been there and seen it. It was breathtaking. My problem was the hotel was £2 million so I had to come up with a good business plan to enable me to get the finance to purchase it. Fortunately for me, I have two very good friends, one a solicitor and his wife a financer. I drafted my business plan with all my research and profit and loss forecasts and prepared to try to find the finance. Unfortunately, due to the nature of the business it wasn't something your average High Street bank would lend on, so my lender had to be specialist. My friends have never let me down in the past and they are phenomenal at finding the right finance package. After a lot of hard work, they eventually found the company to finance it. It was a complicated finance deal as the guy who owned the business I was purchasing was particularly difficult. It took us about nine weeks to seal the deal. The hotel was housed as an asset under the company Round Clock Limited. I was using the house and land as part exchange for the property. The difficulty of the deal was the owner of Croydon Hall didn't want to take ownership of the part exchange and wanted me to remain the owner with him having 100% first charge over it. This left me with the responsibility of selling it and paying him his money. This was most unusual, but my solicitors managed to draft the contract and so the deal was done.

The hotel was in bad repair and needed a lot of work. This wasn't a problem because I had to gut it anyway to turn it into the hotel and club I visualised. My experience in project management from Algeria stood me in good stead for this task. I made a plan of refurbishment which was very rigourous as I wanted to be up and running within three months. particularly as my outgoings were some £10,000 plus a month, so time was money – we needed to open and start earning as soon as possible. The good thing is, I'm an electrician and my friend's partner was a carpenter so between us we could do most of the work ourselves. We hired 12 other guys ranging from painters and decorators to carpenters and builders. My brother came over from Belgium and stayed for a couple of weeks to help us out, which was a great help. We started the project and agreed with everyone we would be working seven days a week until the project was finished and we hit it hard. We started in November and wanted to open for New Year's Eve. This we achieved. The hotel was a standalone building and beside it there was a very large U-shaped coach house with seven bedrooms. This was used as our private accommodation. There was also a lot of work to do there to divide it into two homes, one for myself and one for my friends. There was also a very large barn which we used to store all the old hotel bedding and furniture that we eventually gave to the British Heart Foundation. There were some 30-odd beds and furniture that had been in the hotel rooms previous to our takeover; it took six British Heart Foundation lorries to move the furniture, but it was nice knowing it was going to people that needed it.

Our New Year's opening party was a masquerade and although not packed, we did have a lot of people turn up considering it was our first event. The refurbishment of the hotel was first class. It was stunning and the decor second to none, we often had nice compliments and reviews on the place, and we were proud to own it. On top of this we had to have a website designed and integrated within the website we wanted a dating app similar to Fab swingers, this way our members could communicate with each other and talk about the events, and it opened up a meeting platform. I based the concept of the hotel very similar to Fun4two. You had to be a member to gain entrance. The rules were strict and any problems, you would be banned for life. No second chances. There was a dress code, and we had themed nights like Fun4two. We had a theme song whereby everyone would have to strip down to their underwear. Our song was "You can leave your hat on" by Tom Jones; this worked well putting everyone in the same environment. We had the large Jacuzzi, the sauna and all the playrooms as good if not better than Fun4two. I called it Disney World for adults.

When I took over Croydon Hall, I invited all the neighbours around for tea and cakes to explain what I would be doing with the building. All of them were very supportive, except one couple who were not happy at the concept of having a swingers' club in the area. This came as a bit of a surprise, particularly as the couple in question didn't actually live in the area but they did own a property that they rented on Airbnb. Their property was out of sight from the hotel and around 300 metres away surrounded by woodland. I even explained to them that I could fill their property every weekend, but they turned their noses up at the thought of swingers staying in their Airbnb. They still objected. This caused me a bit of a headache as the hotel was actually within the national park and the couple in question were very friendly with the national park people. They started to try and build up objections to the use of the hotel. This was an interesting challenge for me because although being a little prudish in Britain, we cannot be prejudiced against others' beliefs. My first challenge was with the local police licensing officer. This was a young female police officer whom I had never as yet met. I received a phone call from her requesting that she visit the site to check I was within the law on the licensing side. She expressed that she was not happy about the nature of my venture. Her words were this is just going to be a dirty old man's club. Obviously, I objected to this and informed her that as the licensing officer she cannot have an opinion, she must stick to the rules of the licensing law and if I'm within that then that's as far as she needs to be involved. We arranged a date and time for her and one of her sergeants to come and visit the hotel. I was prepared for a confrontational visit. But to my surprise after we had a walk around and looked at everything, she completely changed her view, so much so that she apologised to me and said she had a different picture in her mind and complimented me on the decor and feel of the hotel ambience.

It always fascinates me how people form opinions based on what they think, but once they visit or understand completely change their views on this lifestyle. I had lots of people contact me about the club in the local area and a lot of people from the local area became members. I had the local MP, counsellors, doctors, solicitors and a large range of people becoming members. On a weekend event the car park was often full of high-end cars like Ferrari, Porsche, Aston Martin to name just a few. Since looking into this lifestyle,

I've had a lot of people come out of the woodwork. People I didn't even realise were in the lifestyle until they found out about the club. I have learned so much about the lifestyle. Obviously, it's each to their own but in my research I found that when you evaluated the success of couples staying together, the couples in this lifestyle had a far lower divorce rate than those outside the lifestyle. When you think about it though, the majority of divorces stem from money troubles or infidelity, couples having hidden desires or fantasies but too scared to talk to their partners. In the swinger lifestyle this is not an issue because these things are in the open and discussed openly so the result being a strong understanding. The seven-year itch is shared as opposed to done sneakily being deceitful. It makes logical sense.

My battle with the National Park was still ongoing though. They failed to win the argument that I had changed the use of the hotel into a club. That was not the case, it was still a hotel and Monday to Friday was advertised as a hotel. The club side was set up as a separate business called Exclusively Silks. The hotel was hired at the weekend by Exclusively Silks in exactly the same way a rugby club could hire the bar, or a wedding could hire the hotel. So, it became very difficult for the National Park to find some excuse to close us down as we were not breaking any laws. They had to be very careful not to be prejudiced against the nature of the club.

Obviously, my objectors stirred up a lot of interest in the place and all of the local papers were making stories out of the new business. I remember some photos that had been taken by the press with long range focus lenses trying to peer into the club which always made me laugh because all they needed to do was knock on the door and they would've been invited in. We had nothing to hide.

My next challenge was when I wanted to extend my licence to 4am on club nights. Obviously, this required a meeting with the city council. It was during this time that I received a phone call from the Daily Mail expressing that they had seen a lot of interest with the local papers and gazettes about the club but did not see any feedback from me. No, I said, nobody has actually come and spoken to me. They asked if they could come and do an exposé on what I was doing. The date they wanted to come was on the same date that I had my hearing for my licence extension. They assured me that they would be finished prior to me going to the hearing. Of course, I had nothing to hide so I was more than happy for them to come and do an exposé. They arrived promptly at 8 o'clock in the morning with the photographer and the journalist and we went through the hotel room by room, the club, how it was run, a bit of history on me and they were thoroughly enjoying their time at the hotel. The interview had taken a lot longer than they had expected And I said I must now go to my hearing to extend my licence. They asked if it would be possible to join me, to which I said of course, no problem.

The hearing turned out to be quite an interesting hearing. The couple who had objected had managed to drum up nine other people to object to the extension of my licence. So, without the Daily Mail reporters, I would've been sat in a room by myself with nine objectors and the city councillors to battle with. You should have seen the faces on the councillors as we went round the desk introducing everyone when suddenly they came across the reporters when they said they were reporters from the Daily Mail the faces on the councillors just dropped. To top it all we had the police representative which was the lady licensing officer and her sergeant present.

We discussed in depth my reasons for the late licence and the objectors put their point forward too, although most of what they said was unsubstantiated. Finally, the councillors turned to the police and asked if they had any objections and what their opinion was. You could have picked me off the floor when she started to talk. I would've definitely said they would've had some sort of objection but no, on the contrary. The police officer stood up and addressed the objectors. Her advice was quite simple. She explained that I don't actually need an extended licence because the licence of a hotel bar is 24 hours and that is extended to guests at the invitation of guests staying at the hotel. This means that the hotel was not under the scrutiny of the police; however, if the licence extension was granted then the police would have a better say on how it was controlled. Needless to say, I got my extension. On top of this I had a double cente page spread in the Daily Mail which has got to be £20,000 of advertising. I also appeared on Loose Women and again on BBC radio. So, all in all, a successful advertising campaign out of nothing!

We were finally starting to get established when out of the blue we hit another problem. My partner's husband suddenly decided he didn't want to be involved anymore; in fact, he had been seeing one of the bar girls. This came as somewhat of a shock to both his wife and myself and was not what we needed at this time of the project. For the next week or two everything was very strained, he had packed up and left and she was constantly crying and distressed. After a few weeks of this, she sat down and had a discussion with me. She said not to worry, she would continue with the project and still sell the house to help fund us till we got fully established. They had two children, a daughter of four and a son of eight. I explained that I was not 100% comfortable with this, after all I am not Dad and neither of us know whether this will succeed or not. My advice was for her to go back to Plymouth and move back into the family home as her husband could not take this from her. He would have to provide a roof over her head. This was agreed and I helped her move back into the family home.

This left me totally alone with a massive project to try and succeed. I was fortunate to have plenty of friends to help, but it was still very nerve wracking and very difficult. It was becoming very difficult to do everything alone and I was wearing myself thin. I remember my father coming over from Thailand and he pulled me to one side and said have you looked at yourself in the mirror lately, you look grey – you need to sell up before this damages your health. It was a few weeks after this that the dreaded pandemic hit us. Covid. Nightmare.

Figure 94 Croydon Hall Aerial Photo

Figure 95 Rear View Croydon Hall

Figure 96 Croydon Hall Front Door

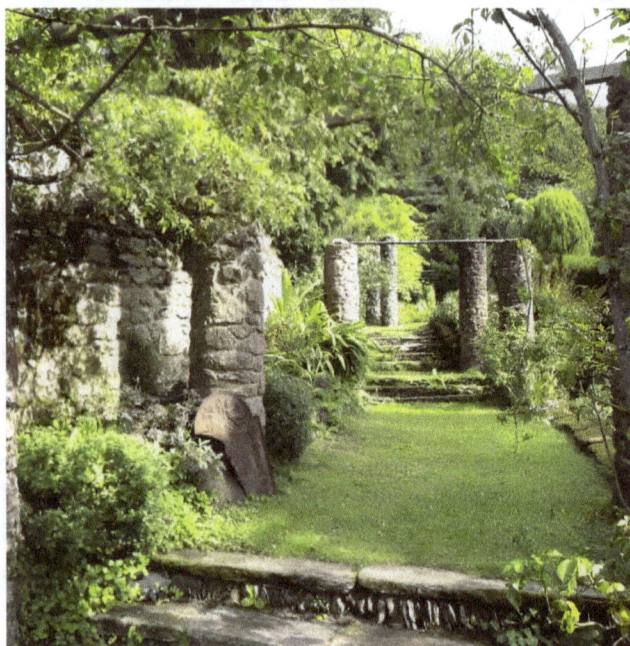

Figure 97 Gardens Croydon Hall

Figure 98 Spa Room

Figure 99 Dance Floor

Figure 100 Bar

So, I now find myself with a two-million-pound hotel plus the house and the land to try and sell. Nothing coming in but still having to pay the loan. I had not been trading long and had no books to show earnings, which meant I was not eligible for any government help.

My saving grace was the deal which the seller had pushed for, leaving me as the owner of the house and land to sell meant I could move back into it. This is what I did and then I put the hotel up for sale. Unfortunately, I was getting nowhere – after all, the leisure industry was in all intents and purposes finished, no one was buying in this industry, particularly with Covid. I had no choice but to try and auction the hotel. Unfortunately, it didn't even meet the bottom price which at the time was only just enough to cover the loan. This unfortunately meant I might have to look at the option of bankruptcy, not something I relished doing.

Then out of the blue, I received a phone call from a guy called Jeremy from a company called Pure Group. He has the contract in the UK for the Henley Regatta. Unfortunately, this was cancelled due to Covid. He had all his staff over here in the UK, unable to fly them back abroad to his hotels. As a result, he was stuck with plenty of manpower but nothing for them to do. Having looked at my hotel, he decided he wanted to buy it so that he could renovate it and utilise his men whilst they were over here in the UK. He had done his homework and knew that I hadn't met the bottom price at the auction, so he made me an offer, albeit a very poor offer. I had to consider it as it meant I might not have to go bankrupt. So, I took it with open arms. The deal, however, was that he would be unable to pay me my money until he was in a position to refinance the hotel. This seemed fair enough – after all, nobody knew what was happening with the pandemic and I understood he had to change it from the club to a boutique hotel and needed the money to do that.

So, we agreed that he would take over my loan payments and once he refinanced, he would pay me what was due. I contacted my lenders and explained the situation and they said they would come back to me with a decision. For me it was a no-brainer. I was already behind on my payments, and it looked very much like I might have to go into bankruptcy so for someone to take over the payments and take over the loan had to be good for the lender, or so I thought. To my surprise the lender came back and said they were unable to agree to the deal because their policy was, they could only fund 50% loan to value so if he was purchasing the hotel for a lot less, than he would have to pay back the majority of the loan to enable him to take over. This to me is crazy and I explained if I go bankrupt the official receiver will take the hotel and sell it for next to nothing and they will lose out heavily. This, however, did not change their decision.

I explained this to Jeremy, and he asked me to send over my contract and he would have a look at it. He came back the following day and explained that when I had bought the hotel, I had actually bought the business and the hotel was an asset of that business. I was the sole director of the business with 1200 shares at £1 each. He would buy 100% of my shares for £1200 and I would resign as director; he would then take over the company and deal with the finance company. I sent a copy of the contract over to my solicitors just to confirm that this could be done and to my bewilderment and theirs there was nothing in the contract that said we couldn't sell my shares. So, this is what we did. I resigned as director. He became director and now owned the company and its assets which included the hotel. The finance company was not overly impressed with me, but in the end, it was the sensible way forward for everyone.

Finally, I had managed to offload the hotel without having to go bankrupt, but I still had the house and land to sell in order to pay the guy I'd bought the hotel from.

When I'd bought the land, I'd obtained planning permission to build three one-million-pound houses. As explained previously we'd managed to build one before the downturn of the construction industry. My thoughts were now if I could build the other two, I might be able to get out of this reasonably unscathed. My issue was although I was the owner by name, the guy I'd bought the hotel from had first charge, which meant he had a say in what I could do with the land.

I collated all my pricing and build costs and even got the finance organised to build then sent the proposal over to the charge holder for approval. He came back negatively and decided it was too much risk for him to take, his reason behind this was that the finance company would have to take a second charge on the property, and he did not like this.

Building the two properties was critical to me getting back on my feet – failing that I would be starting again with nothing to my name, so my plan was to try and find somebody to sell the land to. Someone who would partner with me to build the two units I had planning permission for. This was difficult as most building companies wanted to buy the land for them to build on, not to share the build profits. I met with a friend of mine and his wife who showed interest in the project. He was a carpenter so had a good idea of the build project. We opted to reapply for planning but instead of building two £1.4 million houses we would build four smaller houses as they would be easier to sell. Discussions with our architect suggested that this would be easy to get through planning because of the affordability of the properties. So off we went, we completed all the engineering works and applied for planning. I managed to get the finance based on the planning permission going ahead and my architect, who was one of the best in Plymouth, was 98% sure this would sail through. My friend, however, did not have enough money to buy the land outright and we were relying on the other finance to complete the purchase. In order to seal the deal and secure the land, my friend put down a large deposit and exchanged contracts. We had a specialist planning consultant plus the best architects, and everyone was so confident in the planning coming through. To everyone's amazement, the planners decided they were not happy with four properties and wanted to reduce the number to three. This didn't work for us because our finance company required four properties to make the exercise viable to them. This put us in a very difficult position because we had exchanged contracts which meant the deposit would be lost if we didn't follow through with the purchase. My so-called friend then decided he would find his own builder to invest in and just buy the land and count me out; this was not part of my plan and was not a nice thing to do. It's amazing what money does to people. I am very much a man of my word and if I made a deal with somebody, I would not relinquish that deal. Friends indeed. In the light of day it was purely greed at the thought of profit that they were interested in.

I was explaining my situation to another couple I know, who were friends of mine, and they suggested they had a friend who might be interested in taking the project forward with me. So once again, I went through the project details with the couple and their colleague. They agreed to buy the land and then we would build out together and share the profit equally. Finally, it was coming together. The deal was done, and they purchased the land. I was excited at the prospect of perhaps getting out of this predicament with at least something. But alas, to my utter amazement, about two weeks after completion my friends asked me to meet them at a pub halfway between mine and theirs. This rang alarm bells for me because every time we had met, we always came to my house. My concerns were confirmed when we met, and they said they no longer wanted to build. However, they were happy to sell the land back to me at £100,000 more than they had purchased it for. Can you believe such a con by people you thought were friends? Turns out they just wanted to make a quick buck at my expense. They knew I was in a pickle and took advantage of it. I hate to say it but at the time if I had a gun I'd have done the time for such low lifes, people like that are inhuman — how could you hit a man when he's down? It has been music to my ears that they have been unable to sell it to date.

That left me with the house still to sell. I had previously had a buyer who was prepared to pay £1 million for the house, but the person who had first charge pushed too hard and tried to make a quick aggressive sale which frightened the buyers away. Fortunately for me, we became good friends and consequently I sold the house to them but at a lot cheaper price further down the line. I managed to convince the first charge holder to accept the offer as full and final payment. If not, I would have no alternative but to go bankrupt and the house would fall to the official receiver, and they might not get as much. This got me out of trouble. I ended up with a clean slate, not having to go bankrupt but still having to start again with nothing to my name.

When I look back at my life's experiences this has to be a bitter unfortunate twist at the end. How do I pick myself up from this?

If there was ever a reason why people should consider a trade as a career this would be a fine example. As explained at the beginning of this story, when I left school l took a trade as an electrician. Then when I left the Services, I fell back on my trade which landed me in oil and gas. And here I am once again fortunate to be able to fall back onto my tools to try and earn a living at the bottom of the ladder.

I was also fortunate enough to meet a lovely young lady who moved in with me and we rented a nice, thatched cottage in Kingsteignton, a lovely little town in Devon. I started to build up a business again and I started to teach her to become an electrician just like I had to my brother many moons ago. She was doing exceptionally well, and we worked well together. We stayed together for about three years then she decided she wanted to foster children. This wasn't for me. I was too old now to take on this type of responsibility so after much discussion it was time for us to part. Once again, I found myself isolated and alone, having to start afresh. I was deciding what to do with my life having hit another low point when I received a phone call from my sister saying before I make any decisions on where to move, why don't I come to stay with her and her husband and take some time out, after all I've been through – she wanted to help me out for a change. After a lot of thought and some persuasion from her and my father, I agreed to move to West Sussex and try to start over. The problem for me is I have three wonderful West Highland Terriers which I have accumulated and having had them since puppies they are part of the baggage that come with me. After all, I took responsibility for them so I will take care of them till their dying day. Hamish is now ten, Angus is eight and wee Dougal just two. To be honest they are the only things that give me joy every day. Every time I see them; they are without a shadow of a doubt man's best friend. However, despite the discussions, I think it played heavy on my sister and amongst other things best not to mention we fell out and I once again found myself in a strange town, isolated, trying to make ends meet.

When you're down on luck, alone and isolated, you look at your past. I looked at all the falling outs I've had and questioned whether I was the common denominator. No, I've always helped people, been kind and supportive to the best of my abilities. I concluded that I can rest easy when my time comes in the knowledge that I've lived life to the full and done my best by the people I've interacted with and held true to my principles, and I would do it all again exactly the same way. Life is for living. You're a long time dead.

I've seen enough to know that life
isn't about playing it safe.
It's not about ticking boxes or just getting by.
It's about the moments that make your
heart race, the risks, the falls, the ones
who stayed, and the ones who didn't.
I've loved hard, lost deeply, laughed until it hurt.
I've faced things that broke me, and still, I got
back up. Through it all, I've realised one thing:
I don't want a life I can simply live with.
I want a life that means something.
A life that stirs something in me.
A life that's messy, honest, and mine.
One story to leave behind —
then let it be a life I truly lived.

I was told on many occasions: Allen, you should write a book about all your experiences. Well, here it is. I'm quite sure I still have many more experiences to come, and I look forward to what else life can throw at me. So far, I have had an amazing innings. Long may it continue.

Figure 101 Allen, Hamish, Angus & Dougal

✳ ✳ ✳